THE PASTA COOKBOOK

AUDREY ELLIS

A Martin Book

Published by Martin Books
8 Market Passage, Cambridge CB2 3PF
in association with Pasta Foods Limited
224 London Road, St Albans, Herts AL1 1JF

First published 1980
© Pasta Foods Limited and Audrey Ellis 1980
ISBN 0 85941 145 1

Conditions of sale
All rights reserved. No part of this publication may be reproduced, stored in a retrieval system or transmitted, in any form or by any means, electronic, mechanical, photocopying, recording or otherwise, without the prior permission of the copyright owners.

Featured on the cover are Fried turkey breasts with noodles (page 25), Herbed chicken salad (page 49) and Saffron fish shells (page 89).

Cover picture and photographs on pages 7, 15, 27, 31, 39, 47, 51, 55, 67, 75, 95 by John Lee, the remainder are from the Pasta Information Centre.

Design by Ken Vail
Typesetting by A-Line Services, Saffron Walden
Printed and bound in Great Britain by
Morrison & Gibb Limited, Edinburgh

Foreword

by K L Spencer
Marketing Director, Pasta Foods Limited

Pasta is a very versatile and nutritious food, which is both attractive to serve and good to eat. With the rising cost of high protein foods such as meat, fish, eggs, etc., it not only serves as a cost-reducing ingredient in meals, but also has the benefit of attractive presentation which is stimulating to the appetite. Pasta, such as Record made from Durum wheat with its 12 per cent protein, gives a very nicely balanced food profile.

It is strange that in Britain consumption of pasta is low, compared with that of France and Italy. Obviously, with the right presentation, there is considerable scope for the British housewife to add some additional interest and variety to her family's meals by the judicious use of this interesting ingredient.

The author has used national and traditional local specialities from the British range of foods to complement the exciting shapes and types of Record pasta. Particularly interesting must be the sections on whole wheat products which are finding increasing acceptance, following the overwhelming evidence that they have many dietary advantages.

Audrey Ellis, with her genius for constructing both practical and interesting dishes, was commissioned to write this book and it is sincerely hoped that her recipes will help to provide a new dimension in eating, adding both to the enjoyment of the cook and of the whole family.

Ken Spencer

Contents

Foreword 3

Introduction 6

1 GREAT BRITISH PASTA MEALS 11
Hearty Soups
Coconut soup with lemon floats 12
Smoked fish chowder 13
Cheddar cheese soup 13
Chilli beef soup 14
Quick-cook vegetable soup 16
Chicken and almond soup 16
Rich kidney soup 17
Curried apple and corn soup 18
Main Dishes
Chicken with apples and cider 19
Tuna macaroni bake 20
Hasty cod and lobster casserole 20
Meatballs in broth 21
Beefy pudding 22
Roly poly ham 24
Liver stroganoodle 24
Fried turkey breasts with noodles 25
Carrot and pasta bake 26
Paprika veal with caraway shells 28
Egg noodle ring 28
Mushroom cream pasta with sausages 29
Layered noodle hot-pot 30
Lightning bolognaise sauce 32
Wine glazed chicken platter 32
Devilled kidneys 33
Chicken liver lasagne 34
Smothered lamb 36
Kids' Corner
Supper toasties 37
Sausage and soup pasta 37
Pasta 'n bean bake 38
Sardines in hiding 40
Mandarin magic 40
Chocolate brittle 41

2 SLIMMING SUCCESSFULLY WITH PASTA 42
Light Soups
Chopped chicken and prawn soup 43
Egg and lemon soup 43
Lettuce and pea soup 44
Beetroot soup with dill 45
Super Salads
Cucumber drum salad 46
Frankfurter summer salad 48
Pasta and garlic sausage salad 48
Herbed chicken salad 49
Edam and grape platter 50
Low Calorie Dishes
Fennel and ham gratin 52
Fish in spinach sauce 53
Cottage cheese omelette 54
Baked chicken custard 56

3 FULL-VALUE VEGETARIAN DISHES 57
Peanut pasta burgers 58

Vegetable fritters with lemon sauce   60
Curried egg caramelle   61
Macaroni and aubergine pie   62
Vegetarian lasagne verdi   64
Spaghetti with lentil sauce   65
Hot cheesey squares   65
Blushing beetroot salad   66
Apricot and cucumber salad   67
Pasta beignets with sunrise sauce   68
Leek and cheese special   69
Cauliflower with peanut butter pasta   70

4 INSPIRED PASTA PUDDINGS   71
Everyday Puddings and Desserts
Orange butterscotch shells   72
Prune and pasta delight   73
Ring puffs with cherry sauce   73
Lemon meringue pasta   74
Jamaican custard pudding   76
Fruited noodle puff   76
Exotic Puddings and Desserts
Peach upside-down pudding   78
Honeyed banana noodles   79
Chocolate macaroni meringue   80
Vermicelli ring with rich plum sauce   80
Banana-berry cream   81
Macaroni applecake   82

5 SPOTLIGHT ON PASTA PARTIES   84
Gourmet Dinner Menus
Spaghetti with Stilton and bacon   85
Mimosa pasta salads   88
Saffron fish shells   89
Penny-wise Entertaining
Oven barbecued sausages with orange twistetti salad   90
Curried sausage spaghetti   91
Pork and pasta chow   92
Sesame chicken   93

Introduction

Pasta is surely the most adaptable of all staple foods. It makes a happy marriage with savoury sauces, meat, fish, poultry, eggs, cheese and vegetables. Yet it is equally compatible with the flavours of fresh fruit and creamy desserts. You need never get tired of using your favourite pasta recipes because there is a vast range of shapes to choose from. Substitute wheels for rigatoni, or spirals for short-cut macaroni; just make sure the particular pasta you use is cooked long enough to make it tender and the changes you can ring are endless.

Today it is no longer thought that Marco Polo was responsible for introducing pasta to Europe from the Far East because it was already well known in Italy before his epic travels in China. Even the ancient Egyptians, it seems, used to eat noodles.

What pasta is made of and how

All good quality pasta is made from Durum semolina milled from hard Durum wheat. Softer and less expensive wheats produce a pasta which is recognisable because it leaves the cooking water cloudy and becomes rather tasteless when fully cooked, entirely lacking the delicious nutty flavour and firm texture of the best Durum pasta like Record. People who have only experienced the taste and texture of canned spaghetti find 'the real thing' a revelation in enjoyment.

The method of manufacture is simple, but the correct conditions are vitally important. The dough is extruded through dies which produce the long tubes or ribbons of pasta, automatically cut in convenient lengths and hung up to dry; or cut into

Crisply fried noodles

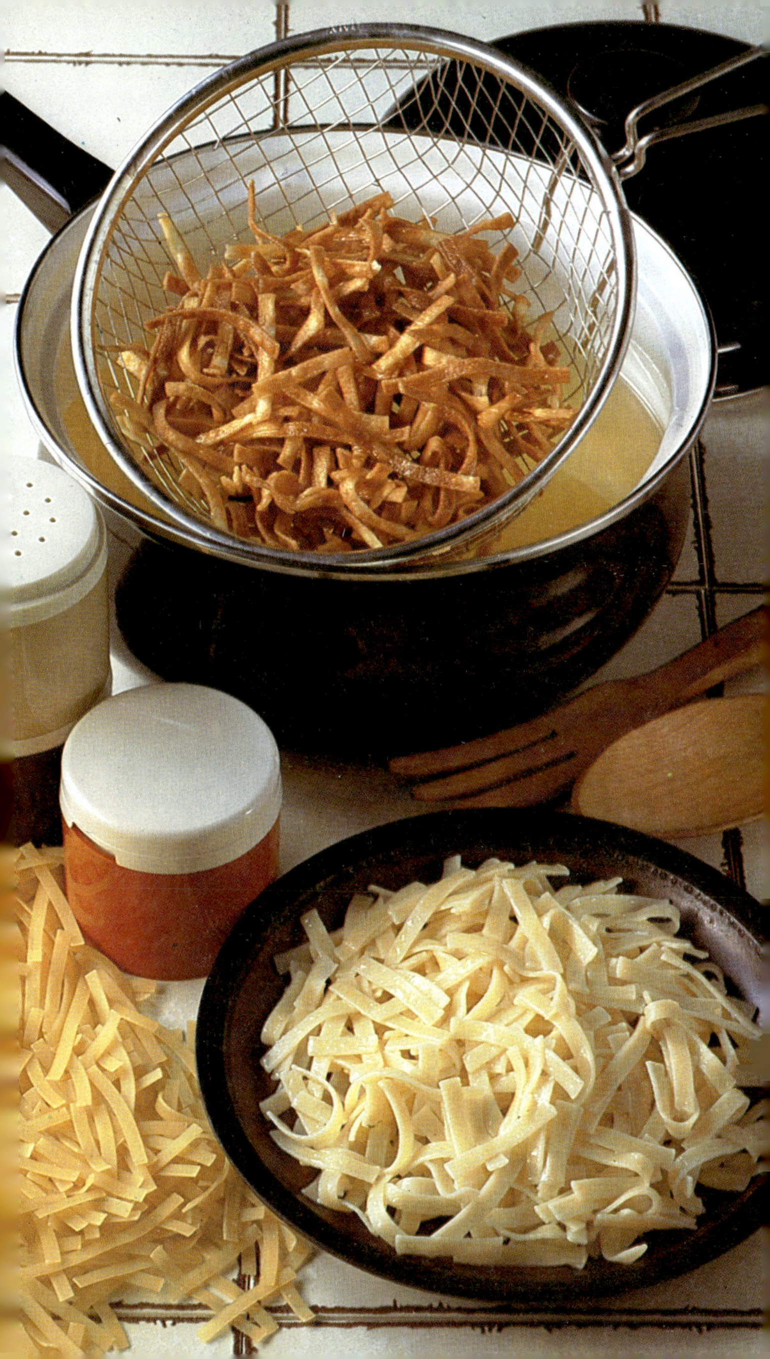

individual shapes such as shells of various sizes, which are dried off on trays. The humidity and temperature of the air in the factory are controlled to ensure the perfect result. A proportion of egg is added to the dough for some shapes, and this gives a higher nutritional value and beautiful rich yellow colour, as well as a more delicate flavour. Look out for egg noodles, vermicelli and lasagne when you are shopping. They cost very little more but the difference in taste is appreciable. Green pasta is produced by adding spinach to the dough and nothing looks more exciting than a layered lasagne blending the colours of a golden cheese sauce with pale green pasta and a rich, russet, meat and tomato sauce.

The food value of pasta
The best quality pasta has a protein content of 12 per cent or more in its uncooked form. This makes it a valuable part of any meal. But since modern eating patterns have accustomed us to insist on highly refined foods, there is a serious lack of roughage in our traditional diet. To stay healthy, most people need to include more dietary fibre in their selection of food, particularly cereal fibre. Whole wheat products include the husk of the grain and that is where the all-important fibre is found. Whole wheat pasta is not just good to eat, it is delicious; children, particularly, enjoy its hearty flavour and biscuity colour.

To most slimmers, the idea of low-calorie cooking would outlaw the inclusion of pasta. But in fact, weight for weight, cooked pasta contains only a few more calories than boiled potato and considerably fewer than plain rice. It is an interesting alternative to starchy vegetables, rice and dried pulses. Unlike any root vegetable, it has no wasteful peel, no damaged portions to be discarded, and has a long storage life. It requires no soaking before cooking like dried pulses, and has a definite advantage over rice in that each shape or strand stays separate when cooked. We are still rather timid in exploiting pasta as part of a conventional meal. Why not pork chop, peas and pasta as a change from potatoes?

How to cook pasta perfectly
Remembering that pasta trebles in weight and volume during the cooking process, use a pan that is large enough to contain a lot of water. You really do need 2.25 litres/4 pints of fast boiling water, with 2 teaspoons salt added, to cook each 225 g/8 oz of pasta. If you add a teaspoon of oil to the water, the strands or shapes will not stick together. Let the water come fully to the boil and then coil long lengths of spaghetti or macaroni as they soften, or sprinkle shapes, into it. Stir gently and boil without a lid on the pan until a small piece tastes firm but not hard. Timings are given on all Record pasta packs as a guide, but do test for yourself. Drain well through a colander. There is no need to rinse unless you intend to use the cooked pasta for salads, or to reheat it later. For these purposes, run cold water through it in the colander, drain well again and use or refrigerate in a polythene container. It keeps well for up to three days. If the cooked pasta is not to be combined with a sauce, melt a small knob of butter in the hot saucepan, or add a teaspoon of oil, return the pasta, season and stir lightly to coat the surfaces with an attractive glisten.

Crisply fried pasta Any small cooked pasta shapes (or long strands, such as spaghetti or macaroni, snipped into short lengths) can easily be deep fried. Use a wire frying basket which neatly fits the chosen pan. Heat 5 cm/2 in. of oil to moderately hot (180° C/360° F) or test by putting in one piece of pasta, which should immediately frizzle and turn golden brown within 30 seconds. Fry the pasta in small batches and drain on soft kitchen paper. Serve tossed in coarsely ground salt, or paprika pepper. Fried pasta makes a delicious garnish for soups, or a party nibble instead of salted nuts.

Saving time on made-up dishes If the recipe calls for oven cooking for at least 45 minutes, and there is plenty of liquid in the other ingredients, you can often layer dry instead of cooked pasta into the dish. It will not only become tender but absorb plenty of tasty flavours during cooking.

Preparing pasta for freezing
To pack cooked pasta, which should be coated with butter or oil as above, divide into serving portions and freeze in polythene containers. To serve, turn directly out of the container into a pan of fast boiling water. Allow the water to return to the boil, separating the pieces gently with a fork. Do not extend the process, otherwise the pasta may become overcooked. Drain well and serve at once.

Dishes which combine pasta with a rich sauce should be frozen in ovenproof containers with seals which can be replaced with sheet foil before reheating. Allow to defrost fully at room temperature first. If the dish includes a separate sauce with the pasta, turn the pasta into the middle of an ovenproof container and pour the sauce round the outside. The sauce takes longer to reheat than the pasta and the moisture from it will prevent the pasta drying out in the oven.

All recipes which are suitable for freezing have been marked with a **F** symbol for easy reference.

Those recipes which are quick to prepare have been marked with a **Q** symbol.

CHAPTER 1

GREAT BRITISH PASTA MEALS

Most people have learned to enjoy the classic Italian approach to pasta, served glistening with oil, crowned with a rich meat or tomato sauce and sprinkled with Parmesan. But I think it high time to introduce appetising and exciting new dishes using more of our own familiar and well loved ingredients, such as fresh pork sausages and Cheddar cheese. This section also includes soups which are a meal in themselves, made more filling and delicious by incorporating pasta in the recipes; and with an eye to the trend towards letting the kids occasionally cater for themselves, here are some simple recipes to give them encouragement.

Hearty Soups

Coconut soup with lemon floats
Serves 4

150 g/5 oz desiccated coconut
300 ml/½ pint water
2 tablespoons oil
4 spring onions, trimmed
1 clove garlic, crushed
1 teaspoon ground turmeric
900 ml/1½ pints chicken stock
1 strip of lemon rind
50 g/2 oz Record vermicelli
100 g/4 oz cooked chicken, diced
salt and pepper
4 slices of lemon

Place 100 g/4 oz of the coconut in a small pan, pour over the water and bring slowly to the boil. Allow to stand until cool then squeeze the coconut to extract as much of the 'milk' as possible from it. Pour through a sieve, squeezing the shreds until really dry.

Heat half the oil in a large saucepan. Chop the onions and add them to the pan with the garlic and turmeric and fry gently until soft. Add the chicken stock, lemon rind and coconut 'milk' and bring to the boil. Cover and simmer for 10 minutes. Add the pasta and continue to cook for a further 5 minutes. Remove the lemon rind, add the chicken to the pan and bring back to the boil. Add salt and pepper to taste.

Meanwhile, fry the remaining coconut in the rest of the oil until golden brown and crisp. Sprinkle over the lemon slices and float 1 slice on each bowl of soup.

Smoked fish chowder
Serves 4

100 g/4 oz streaky bacon, diced
1 large onion, chopped
600 ml/1 pint water
75 g/3 oz Record soup pasta shells
225 g/8 oz smoked cod fillet
600 ml/1 pint milk
salt and black pepper
chopped fresh parsley

Place the bacon dice in a large saucepan over gentle heat until the fat starts to run. Raise the heat and cook until the bacon bits are golden. Add the onion and water and bring to the boil. Stir in the pasta and boil gently for 10 minutes.

At the same time, place the fish and milk in a saucepan and poach gently for 10 minutes. Lift out the fish, reserving the cooking liquid, remove any skin and bones and flake roughly. Add the fish to the pasta mixture and strain in the reserved liquid. Bring back to the boil, cover and simmer for a further 5 minutes. Taste and season with pepper, adding salt only if necessary. Serve hot sprinkled with parsley.

Cheddar cheese soup
Serves 4

25 g/1 oz butter *or* margarine
1 small carrot, grated
1 small onion, grated
½ teaspoon dry mustard
½ teaspoon paprika pepper
900 ml/1½ pints chicken stock
150 ml/¼ pint milk
2 tablespoons Record whole wheat semolina
100 g/4 oz strong Cheddar cheese, grated
salt and pepper
macaroni crisps (*see* page 9)

Melt the butter or margarine in a large saucepan and use to cook the carrot and onion gently until soft. Stir in the mustard, paprika and stock and bring to the boil. Cover and simmer for 15 minutes. Stir in the milk and bring back to boiling point. Sprinkle on the semolina and stir constantly while the soup boils for a further 5 minutes. Add the cheese and season to taste. Stir until the cheese has melted, then remove from the heat and serve each portion very hot and sprinkled with macaroni crisps.

Chilli beef soup **F**
Serves 4

1 tablespoon oil
100 g/4 oz minced beef
100 g/4 oz finely chopped onion
100 g/4 oz finely chopped carrot
½ teaspoon mild chilli powder
½ teaspoon cocoa powder
½ teaspoon salt
1 tablespoon tomato purée
1 beef stock cube, crumbled
900 ml/1½ pints water
1 tablespoon cornflour
150 g/5 oz Record soup pasta shells

Put the oil in a large saucepan, add the minced beef and stir over moderate heat until light brown and crumbly. Add the onion and carrot and cook, stirring, for a further minute. Add the chilli powder, cocoa, salt, tomato purée, stock cube and water. Bring to the boil, stirring occasionally. Cover and simmer for 20 minutes. Moisten the cornflour with a little water. Add the pasta to the soup, bring back to the boil, stir well and blend in the moistened cornflour. Simmer for a further 10 minutes.

Chilli beef soup

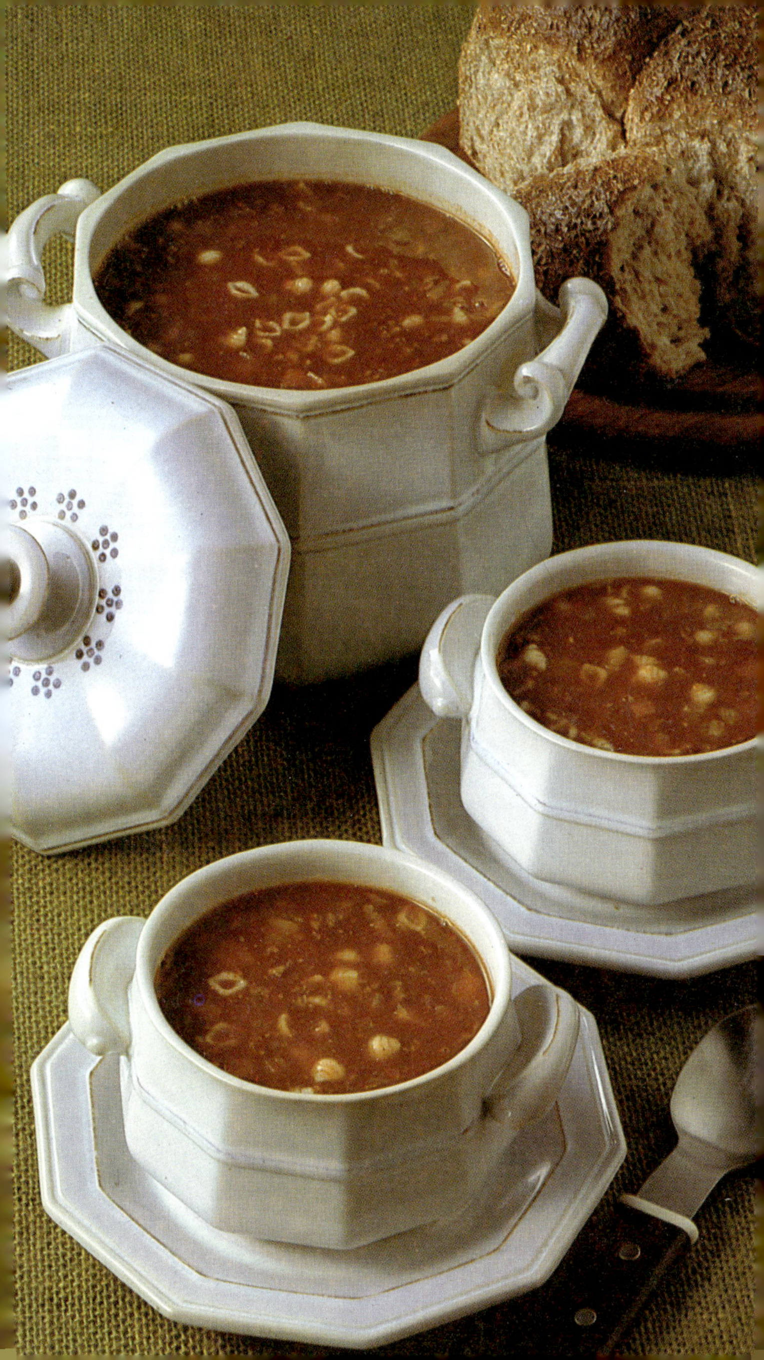

Quick-cook vegetable soup

Serves 4

15 g/½ oz butter *or* margarine
100 g/4 oz coarsely grated onion
100 g/4 oz coarsely grated carrot
100 g/4 oz coarsely grated parsnip
1 chicken stock cube
425 g/15 oz can tomato juice
150 ml/¼ pint water
1 tablespoon chopped parsley
300 ml/½ pint milk
50 g/2 oz Record quick-cook macaroni
salt and pepper

Melt the butter or margarine in a large saucepan, add the onion, carrot and parsnip and stir over moderate heat until the vegetables are soft. Crumble in the stock cube, add the tomato juice, water and parsley and stir well. Bring to the boil, cover and simmer for 10 minutes. Add the milk, bring back to the boil, stir in the pasta and cook gently, covered, for a further 10 minutes, stirring occasionally. Add salt and pepper to taste.

Chicken and almond soup

Serves 4

2 chicken leg portions
4 sticks celery, chopped
1 medium onion, chopped
1 medium parsnip, chopped
2 tablespoons chopped parsley
strip of lemon rind
1 bay leaf
1 litre/1¾ pints water
salt and pepper
25 g/1 oz ground almonds
75 g/3 oz Record tagliatelle
4 tablespoons single cream

Place the chicken portions in a large saucepan with the celery, onion, parsnip, parsley, lemon rind, bay leaf and water. Bring to the boil, add a little salt and pepper, cover and simmer for 45 minutes, or until the vegetables are soft. Lift out the chicken portions. Add the almonds to the pan with the pasta, bring back to boiling point and cook for a further 25 minutes. Meanwhile, remove the flesh from the chicken bones and dice it. Add to the soup and simmer for a further 5 minutes. Remove the bay leaf and lemon rind, adjust the seasoning if necessary and stir in the cream.

Rich kidney soup   **❻**
Serves 4

225 g/8 oz ox kidney
25 g/1 oz butter *or* margarine
1 medium onion, chopped
1 teaspoon dried mixed herbs
900 ml/1½ pints beef stock
150 ml/¼ pint brown ale
100 g/4 oz Record short-cut macaroni
salt and pepper

Finely chop the kidney, discarding any skin and white core. Melt the butter or margarine in a large saucepan and use to fry the onion gently until beginning to soften. Add the kidney, herbs, stock and ale and bring to the boil. Cover and simmer for 1 hour, or until the kidney bits are tender. Add the pasta and stir until boiling. Then cook for a further 15 minutes, or until the pasta is tender. Season well to taste and serve hot.

Curried apple and corn soup

Serves 4

25 g/1 oz butter *or* margarine
1 small onion, chopped
2 teaspoons curry powder
175 g/6 oz prepared cooking apple slices
1 chicken stock cube
300 ml/½ pint milk
300 ml/½ pint water
1 tablespoon lemon juice
50 g/2 oz Record spaghetti rings, cooked
198 g/7 oz can sweetcorn kernels
salt and pepper
4 tablespoons single cream

Melt the butter or margarine in a large saucepan and use to fry the onion gently until soft. Stir in the curry powder and cook, stirring, for 2 minutes. Add the apple slices, crumble in the stock cube and add the milk and water. Bring to the boil, stirring constantly. Cover and simmer for 25 minutes. Liquidise the soup and return it to the pan with the lemon juice, pasta, corn and liquid from the can. Bring to boiling point and season to taste. Serve hot and swirl 1 tablespoon of single cream into each portion in the plate.

Main Dishes

Chicken with apples and cider
Serves 4

2 tablespoons oil
1 large onion, chopped
350 g/12 oz prepared cooking apple slices
1 chicken stock cube
300 ml/½ pint dry cider
50 g/2 oz seedless raisins
1 teaspoon dried dill weed
2 teaspoons cornflour
salt and pepper
175 g/6 oz Record pasta twistetti, cooked
350 g/12 oz cooked chicken, diced
20 g/¾ oz butter *or* margarine, melted

Heat the oil and use to fry the onion and half the apple gently until the onion is soft. Crumble in the stock cube, add the cider, raisins and half the dill weed and bring to the boil, stirring. Cook, uncovered, until the liquid has reduced by about one third. Moisten the cornflour with 2 tablespoons water and add to the pan. Stir until sauce boils and thickens. Taste and add salt and pepper if necessary.

Put about half the pasta in a greased ovenproof dish, top with half the chicken and spoon over the sauce. Repeat these layers once more. Arrange the remaining apple slices, overlapping, on top of the layered ingredients, brush generously with butter and sprinkle with the remaining dill. Bake in a moderate oven (180°C/350°F/Gas Mark 4) for about 25 minutes, until piping hot and the apple topping is tender.

Tuna macaroni bake

Serves 4

75 g/3 oz butter *or* margarine
1 large onion, chopped
50 g/2 oz plain flour
600 ml/1 pint milk
1 teaspoon made English mustard
1 teaspoon salt
black pepper
198 g/7 oz can tuna
3 eggs, hard-boiled
12 stuffed green olives, chopped
225 g/8 oz Record short-cut macaroni, cooked
50 g/2 oz Cheddar cheese, grated

Melt the butter or margarine in a saucepan and use to fry the onion gently until soft. Stir in the flour until well blended. Gradually add the milk and bring to the boil, stirring constantly. Mix in the mustard and salt and add pepper to taste. Drain the liquid from the tuna into the sauce and stir well. Flake the fish and chop the eggs. Place one quarter of the sauce in the base of a medium-size deep ovenproof casserole. Top with one-third of the tuna, egg, olives and pasta. Repeat these layers twice more and finish with a layer of the sauce. Sprinkle over the cheese and bake in a moderately hot oven (200°C/400°F/Gas Mark 6) for 40 minutes, until the top is golden brown.

Hasty cod and lobster casserole

Serves 4

175 g/6 oz Record pasta shells
450 g/1 lb cod fillet
300 ml/½ pint milk
425 g/15 oz can condensed lobster bisque
salt and pepper
chopped fresh parsley

Arrange the dry pasta shells in an even layer in a well-greased ovenproof dish. Remove any skin and bones from the fish and cut it into chunks. Arrange on the pasta. Blend the milk with the bisque, add extra seasoning if wished, and pour over the fish mixture. Cover and cook in a moderate oven (180° C/350°F/Gas Mark 4) for 45 minutes, or until the pasta is cooked. Sprinkle generously with parsley before serving.

Meatballs in broth
Serves 4

1 small onion
100 g/4 oz Record short-cut macaroni, cooked
225 g/8 oz minced beef
225 g/8 oz minced pork
1 teaspoon salt
½ teaspoon pepper
1 teaspoon dried oregano
2 eggs, hard-boiled
about 50 g/2 oz seedless raisins
900 ml/1½ pints strong beef stock
½ teaspoon Worcestershire sauce

Finely chop the onion and half the cooked pasta. Mix with the beef, pork, salt, pepper and oregano. Divide the mixture into 16 portions. Cut the eggs into 16 pieces. Shape each portion of meat into a round, place a piece of egg and one or two raisins in the centre, then bring up the meat mixture to enclose the filling completely. Press to make a round ball.

Heat the stock and Worcestershire sauce in a large saucepan and when it comes to the boil carefully add the meatballs. Bring the liquid to simmering point and allow to bubble gently for about 10 minutes. Add the remaining pasta to the broth and bring back to simmering point. Serve hot in bowls.

Beefy pudding
Serves 6

2 tablespoons oil
1 medium onion, chopped
225 g/8 oz minced beef
300 ml/½ pint beef stock
4 tablespoons tomato ketchup
1 packet (85 g/3 oz) sage and onion stuffing mix
150 g/5 oz Record spaghetti, cooked
2 eggs, beaten
salt and pepper
Sauce
396 g/14 oz can tomatoes
3 tablespoons tomato purée
2 teaspoons sugar
salt and pepper

Heat the oil and use to fry the onion gently until soft. Add the minced beef and fry, stirring, until it looks brown and crumbly. Stir in the stock and ketchup, and bring to the boil. Remove from the heat and add the stuffing mix, pasta and egg. Stir well and season to taste. Turn into a greased generous 1 litre/2 pint pudding basin. Cover with greased foil and steam for 2 hours.

Meanwhile, make the sauce. Drain the tomatoes, reserving the liquid from the can. Roughly chop the tomatoes and place in a small pan with 2 tablespoons of the reserved liquid, the tomato purée and sugar. Season with a little salt and pepper and cook gently for about 10 minutes, stirring frequently. Press the mixture through a sieve and add a little more of the reserved liquid if necessary to give a coating consistency. Check the seasoning and reheat the sauce. Turn out the pudding on to a warm serving dish and spoon over the sauce. Serve with a pepper and tomato salad.

Beefy pudding

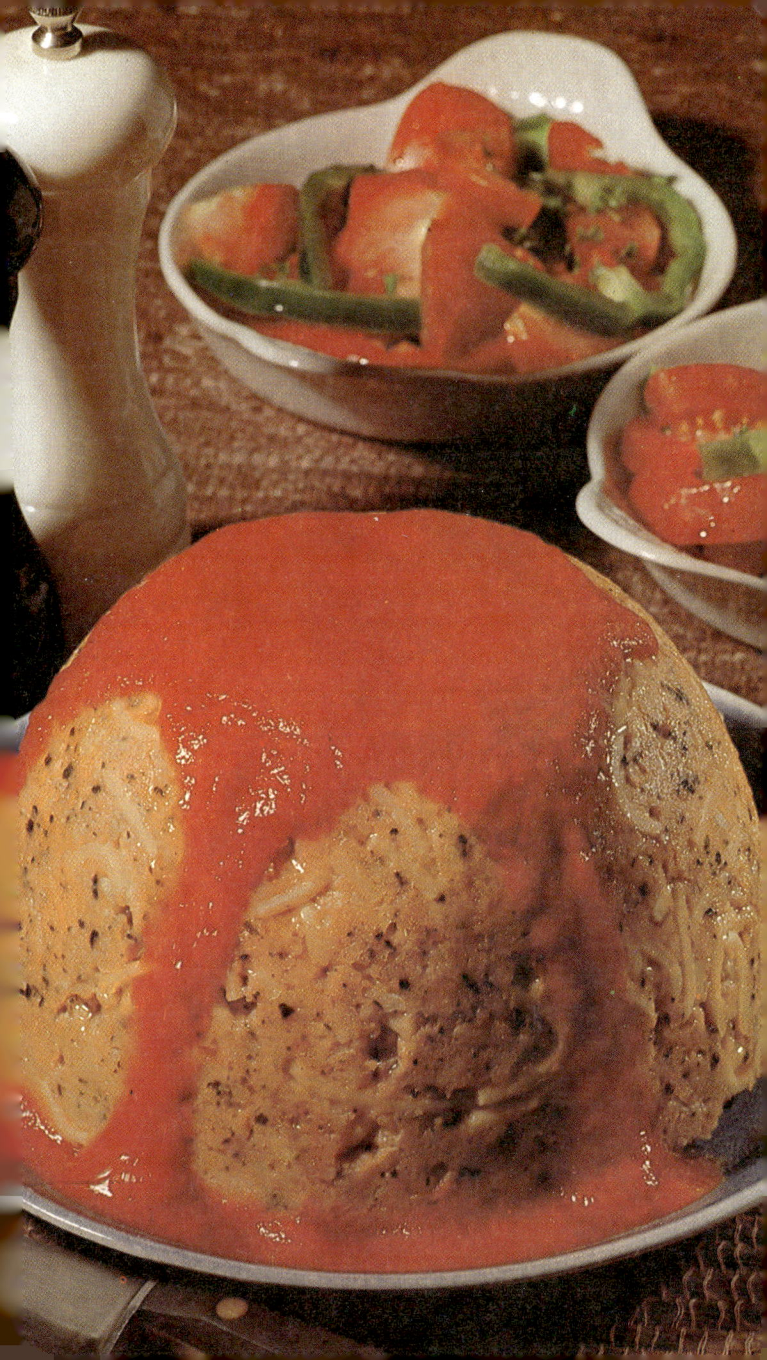

Roly poly ham
Serves 4

175 g/6 oz Record short-cut macaroni, cooked
little yeast extract spread
4 slices ham
3 medium tomatoes, skinned
2 eggs, hard-boiled
25 g/1 oz butter *or* margarine
25 g/1 oz flour
450 ml/¾ pint milk
2 teaspoons tomato purée
75 g/3 oz Cheddar cheese, grated

Place the pasta in the base of a greased ovenproof dish. Spread a little yeast extract over the surface of each slice of ham. Chop the tomatoes and reserve one third. Chop the eggs and mix with two thirds of the tomato. Divide between the slices of ham and roll them up. Arrange the ham rolls on the pasta. Place the butter or margarine, flour and milk in a saucepan and whisk over moderate heat until the sauce boils and thickens. Stir in the reserved tomato, the tomato purée and most of the cheese. Pour the sauce over the ham rolls and pasta. Sprinkle with the remaining cheese and bake in a moderate oven (180°C/350°F/Gas Mark 4) for 15 minutes.

Liver stroganoodle
Serves 4

350 g/12 oz lamb's liver
2 tablespoons plain flour
2 tablespoons oil
1 large onion, chopped
450 ml/¾ pint beef stock
150 g/5 oz Record noodles
298 g/10½ oz can condensed oxtail soup
4 tablespoons soured cream
paprika pepper

Cut the liver into 1.25 cm/½ in. strips and coat in flour. Heat the oil and use to fry the liver strips with the onion until just sealed on all sides and the onion is golden. Meanwhile, place the stock in a saucepan and bring to the boil. Add the pasta and boil gently for 8 minutes. Stir in the soup, then fold in the liver mixture. Transfer to a shallow ovenproof dish, cover and cook in a moderate oven (180°C/350°F/Gas Mark 4) for 30 minutes. Spoon over the soured cream and sprinkle this with paprika before serving.

Fried turkey breasts with noodles
Serves 4

4 turkey breast portions
1 packet seasoned poultry crumb coating
4 tablespoons oil
225 g/8 oz Record egg noodles
chopped parsley
tomato slices
Sauce
25 g/1 oz butter *or* margarine
1 small onion, sliced
450 g/1 lb tomatoes, chopped
1 teaspoon soft brown sugar
150 ml/¼ pint chicken stock
½ teaspoon dried basil
salt and pepper

First make the sauce. Melt the butter or margarine and fry onion until soft. Add the tomatoes, brown sugar, stock and basil. Bring to the boil, cover and simmer for 20 minutes. Add seasoning to taste. Sieve, or liquidise and then sieve the sauce to remove the seeds, return to the pan and keep warm.

While the sauce is simmering, prepare the turkey schnitzels. Beat out thinly between layers of greaseproof paper or cling wrap, and coat on both sides with the crumb mixture. Fry, two at a time, in a frying pan, in the oil, for about 3 minutes on each side, or until golden brown all over.

Meanwhile, cook the noodles. Drain well, transfer to a warm serving dish, arrange the turkey breast schnitzels on top and pour over the sauce. Serve sprinkled with parsley and garnished with tomato slices.

Note The sauce, diluted with equal quantities of chicken stock and milk, makes an excellent soup. Serve garnished with crisply fried noodles (*see* page 9).

Carrot and pasta bake
Serves 4

1 beef stock cube
300 ml/½ pint water
450 g/1 lb pork boiling-ring sausage
3 tablespoons oil
1 large onion, chopped
198 g/7 oz can sweetcorn kernels
2 teaspoons cornflour
225 g/8 oz coarsely grated carrot
175 g/6 oz Record rigatoni, cooked

Make up the stock cube with the water. Cut the sausage into thick diagonal slices. Place 2 tablespoons of the oil in a saucepan and use to fry the onion gently until soft. Add the sausage, corn, liquid from the can and the stock and bring to the boil. Moisten the cornflour with a little cold water and stir into the mixture. Transfer to a shallow ovenproof dish.

Meanwhile, cook the carrot, in just sufficient water to cover, for 5 minutes, or until the liquid is almost all absorbed. Stir in the pasta and spread over the sausage mixture. Trickle over the remaining oil. Cover with foil and cook in a moderately hot oven (190°C/375°F/Gas Mark 5) for 20 minutes.

Carrot and pasta bake

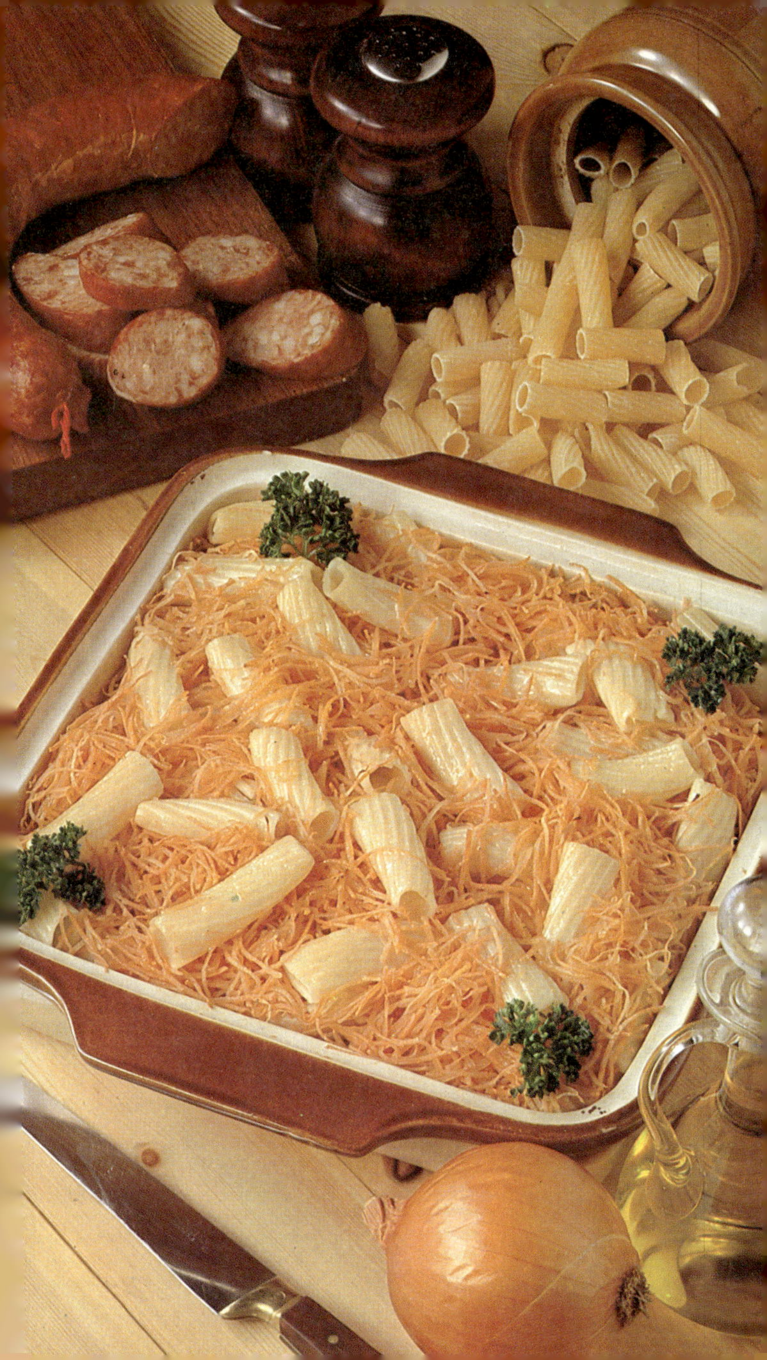

Paprika veal with caraway shells
Serves 4

2 tablespoons oil
1 medium onion, chopped
1 clove garlic, crushed
450 g/1 lb diced pie veal
1 tablespoon sweet paprika pepper
salt and pepper
175 g/6 oz Record pasta shells
100 g/4 oz cottage cheese
150 ml/¼ pint soured cream
15 g/½ oz butter *or* margarine
1 teaspoon caraway seeds
chopped fresh parsley

Heat the oil in a saucepan and use to fry the onion and garlic gently until soft. Add the veal and fry, stirring, until sealed on all sides. Sprinkle in the paprika and add a little salt, stir well, cover and cook gently for about 45 minutes, or until the veal is tender. Meanwhile, cook the pasta.

When the veal is tender, stir in the cottage cheese and soured cream and season well with salt and pepper. Reheat carefully to boiling point. Drain the pasta. Melt the butter or margarine in the hot saucepan used for cooking the pasta, add the caraway seeds, pasta and salt and pepper to taste. Toss together lightly, then turn into a hot, shallow serving dish and spoon the veal mixture on top. Garnish with chopped parsley and serve at once.

Egg noodle ring
Serves 4

200 ml/6 fl oz milk
2 eggs
175 g/6 oz Record egg noodles, cooked
salt and pepper

Heat the milk until bubbles form round the edge of the pan. Whisk the eggs, pour on the hot milk and continue whisking for 30 seconds. Stir in the noodles and season well with salt and pepper. Turn the mixture into a buttered generous 1 litre/2 pint ring mould. Place on a baking sheet and cover lightly with foil. Bake in a moderate oven (170°C/325°F/Gas Mark 3) for 35 minutes, or until firm to the touch. Turn out on a warm serving dish and fill as desired.

Variation Instead of filling the ring with a cooked meat mixture, add 75 g/3 oz grated Gouda or Cheddar cheese to the noodle mixture before cooking. Serve with a simple hot tomato sauce (*see* sauce in recipe for Fried turkey breasts with noodles, page 25) for a lighter meal.

Mushroom cream pasta with sausages
Serves 4

225 g/8 oz Record pasta spirals
25 g/1 oz butter *or* margarine
450 g/1 lb pork and beef chipolata sausages
1 large onion, chopped
100 g/4 oz button mushrooms, sliced
150 ml/¼ pint soured cream
salt and pepper

Cook the pasta. Meanwhile, melt the butter or margarine in a frying pan and use to fry the sausages over moderate heat for about 10 minutes, turning them frequently, until they are cooked and golden brown all over. Remove the sausages from the pan and keep hot. Add the onion and mushrooms to the fat remaining in the pan and fry until onion is golden brown, stirring occasionally. Drain the pasta well, then return it to the saucepan. Add the onion mixture and the cream, mix well and season to taste with salt and pepper. Serve hot with the sausages.

Layered noodle hot-pot
Serves 4

225 g/8 oz minced beef
1 teaspoon salt
½ teaspoon pepper
flour for coating
2 tablespoons oil
225 g/8 oz Record tagliatelle
40 g/1½ oz Cheddar cheese, grated
Sauce
50 g/2 oz can anchovies
1 large onion, chopped
396 g/14 oz can tomatoes
1 tablespoon tomato purée
½ teaspoon dried marjoram
50 g/2 oz stuffed green olives, sliced
salt and pepper

Combine the beef and seasoning and divide the mixture into 16 portions. Shape each into a ball and coat in flour. Heat the oil in a large saucepan and use to fry the meatballs for about 5 minutes, turning them frequently, until browned all over. Drain and keep hot.

Make the sauce in the same pan. Add the oil from the can of anchovies to the juices remaining in the pan and use to cook the onion gently until soft. Add the tomatoes and liquid from the can, the tomato purée and marjoram. Bring to the boil, then cook gently for 15 minutes. Chop the anchovies and stir into the sauce with the olives. Taste and season carefully with pepper, adding salt only if necessary.

Meanwhile, cook the pasta and drain well. Place one third in a greased deep ovenproof dish and cover with half the meatballs then half the sauce. Repeat these layers once and put the rest of the pasta on top. Sprinkle over the cheese and place in a moderately hot oven (190°C/375°F/Gas Mark 5) for 20 minutes. Serve with a green salad.

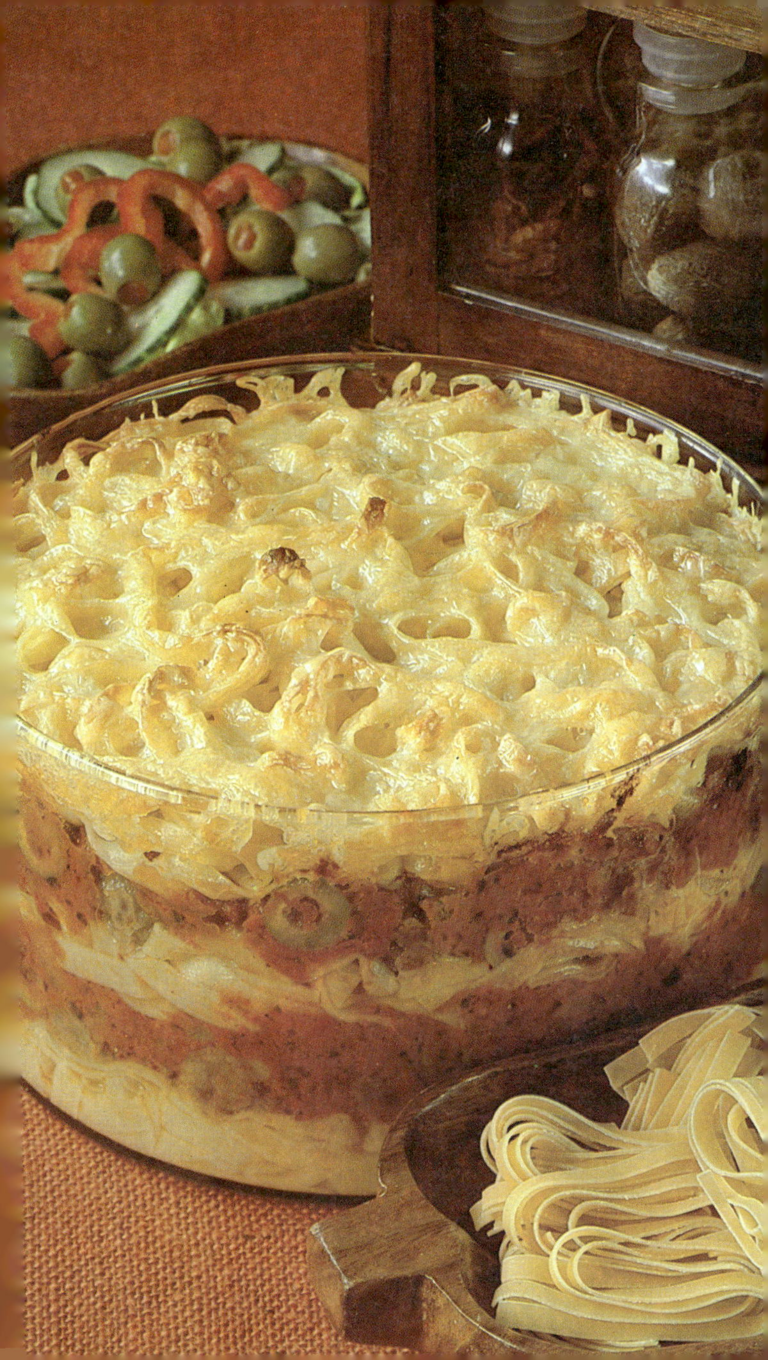

Lightning bolognaise sauce

Serves 4

2 tablespoons oil
225 g/8 oz minced beef
425 g/15 oz can tomato juice
1 tablespoon dried onion flakes
1 beef stock cube
1 teaspoon garlic salt
¼ teaspoon black pepper
½ teaspoon dried oregano
½ teaspoon ground bay leaves

Heat the oil in a saucepan and use to fry the beef lightly, stirring until it turns colour. Add the tomato juice, onion flakes, crumbled stock cube, salt, pepper, oregano and bay leaves. Bring to the boil, stir well, cover and simmer for 30 minutes. Taste and add more seasoning if required.

Spaghetti with sauce This type of pasta served with a rich meat or tomato sauce and sprinkled with Parmesan, has been a favourite inexpensive meal for many years. You can buy prepared sauces in cans or jars, but recipes to make up the sauces at home are sometimes long and complicated. This recipe is a delicious one, suitable to serve over any kind of cooked pasta, which turns it into a nourishing meal with the minimum of effort.

Wine glazed chicken platter

Serves 4

25 g/1 oz butter *or* margarine
3 tablespoons clear honey
2 teaspoons soy sauce
4 chicken portions
5 tablespoons dry red wine
salt and pepper
175 g/6 oz Record rigatoni
78 g/2¾ oz can red pimento
225 g/8 oz hot cooked green peas
sprigs of watercress

Soften the butter or margarine and mix with the honey and soy sauce. Brush the chicken portions with this mixture and arrange them in a roasting tin, skin side downwards. Pour the wine into the tin and place in a hot oven (220°C/425°F/Gas Mark 7) for 20 minutes. Turn the chicken portions, sprinkle with salt and pepper and baste with the juices in the tin. Return to the oven for a further 15 minutes, basting the chicken once more during this time.

Meanwhile, cook the pasta. Drain the pimento, reserving the liquid from the can, and cut into strips. Drain the pasta well, combine with the peas and pimento and fork in the reserved liquid. Arrange on a warm serving platter and top with the chicken portions. Keep warm.

Stir the juices in the roasting tin over moderate heat until slightly reduced and syrupy. Spoon over the chicken to build up the glaze and serve hot, garnished with sprigs of watercress.

Devilled kidneys
Serves 4

450 g/1 lb pig's kidneys
25 g/1 oz plain flour
50 g/2 oz lard *or* dripping
1 clove garlic, crushed
1 large onion, sliced
200 ml/6 fl oz red wine
1 beef stock cube
125 ml/4 fl oz water
2 teaspoons made English mustard
2 teaspoons Worcestershire sauce
salt and pepper
175 g/6 oz Record pasta spirals

Slice the kidneys, discarding the white core, and dust the slices with flour. Melt the lard or dripping and use to fry the garlic and onion until soft. Add the kidney and fry gently for 5 minutes, turning the slices occasionally. Stir in any remaining flour until well blended. Pour over the wine, bring to the boil, stirring constantly, and allow to cook, uncovered, for 3 minutes. Crumble in the stock cube and add the water, mustard and Worcestershire sauce. Stir well, bring back to the boil, cover and simmer for 15 minutes, or until the kidney is tender. Add salt and pepper to taste.

Meanwhile, cook the pasta, drain well and serve plain, spread on a warm dish, with the kidney sauce spooned over, or pour into the centre of an egg noodle ring (*see* page 28).

Chicken liver lasagne 🅕
Serves 4

3 tablespoons oil
2 medium onions, chopped
225 g/8 oz chicken livers
1 clove garlic, crushed
100 g/4 oz ham, chopped
175 g/6 oz mushrooms, chopped
750 ml/1¼ pints chicken stock
3 tablespoons dry sherry
salt and black pepper
175 g/6 oz Record lasagne
25 g/1 oz butter *or* margarine
20 g/¾ oz flour
300 ml/½ pint milk
75 g/3 oz cheese, grated

Heat the oil in a saucepan and use to fry the onion gently until soft. Roughly chop the livers and add to the pan with the garlic. Fry, stirring, until the livers are just firm and starting to brown. Mix in the ham, mushrooms, stock and sherry and bring to the boil. Cover and simmer for 20 minutes. Season well and

Chicken liver lasagne

spoon a layer of the sauce into a greased shallow ovenproof dish. Arrange a single layer of dry pasta on top and spoon over more of the sauce. Continue to make layers of pasta and sauce in this way until both are used up, finishing with a layer of sauce. Cover closely with foil and cook in a moderately hot oven (190°C/375°F/Gas Mark 5) for 30 minutes.

Meanwhile, place the butter or margarine, flour and milk in a small saucepan and whisk over moderate heat until boiling. Season to taste. Remove the foil from the pasta, pour over the white sauce and sprinkle with the cheese. Return the dish to the oven, uncovered, for a further 30 minutes, until golden brown on top.

Smothered lamb
Serves 4

1 medium leek, sliced
450 g/1 lb boned shoulder of lamb, diced
1 large onion, chopped
1 medium carrot, chopped
1 medium parsnip, diced
1 bay leaf
about 600 ml/1 pint chicken stock
175 g/6 oz Record egg lasagne
40 g/1½ oz butter *or* margarine
40 g/1½ oz plain flour
2 teaspoons lemon juice
3 tablespoons chopped mixed herbs (parsley, mint, marjoram, chives)
salt and pepper
1 egg yolk
150 ml/¼ pint single cream

Rinse the leek in a sieve, then place in a saucepan with the lamb, onion, carrot, parsnip, bay leaf and 600 ml/1 pint stock. Bring to the boil, cover and simmer for about 1 hour, or until the meat and vegetables are tender. Meanwhile, cook the pasta. Remove the bay leaf and strain the stock into a measuring jug. Make up to 600 ml/1 pint again with more stock if necessary. Keep meat and vegetables hot.

Melt the butter or margarine in a saucepan and stir in the flour. Cook for 1 minute, then gradually add the measured stock and bring to the boil, stirring constantly, until thickened. Add the lemon juice, 2 tablespoons of the herbs and seasoning to taste. Bring to boiling point again and simmer for 3 minutes. Then beat in the egg yolk and cream and reheat, but do not allow the sauce to boil. Stir in the meat and vegetables.

Drain the pasta and arrange in layers with the meat mixture in a hot serving dish, ending with meat mixture. Sprinkle over the rest of the herbs and serve at once.

Kids' Corner

Supper toasties   ◉
Serves 4

2 lean bacon *or* ham steaks (about 75 g/3 oz each)
1 tablespoon oil
1 medium onion, chopped
198 g/7 oz can baked beans
1 large tomato, chopped
75 g/3 oz Record whole wheat spaghetti rings, cooked
4 slices of bread
parsley sprigs

Cook the steaks under a hot grill for about 4 minutes on each side, or until cooked. Cut into small pieces. Place the oil and onion in a saucepan and cook over moderate heat until the onion is just turning golden brown. Add the baked beans, bacon pieces, tomato and pasta and stir until piping hot. Meanwhile, toast the slices of bread on both sides and place each one on a plate. Spoon on the hot pasta mixture and garnish each toastie with parsley sprigs. Serve at once.

Sausage and soup pasta   ◉
Serves 2

8 thin *or* 4 thick pork sausages
1 tablespoon oil
156 g/5½ oz can condensed green pea soup
75 g/3 oz Record pasta wheels

Snip the skin of the sausages with kitchen scissors, press out the filling and divide into 12 equal pieces. With floured hands, shape each piece into a ball.

Place the oil in a frying pan, add the sausage balls and fry gently for about 10 minutes, turning them frequently until cooked and golden brown all over. While the sausage balls are frying, cook the pasta. Add the contents of the can of soup to the frying pan and stir until the mixture is piping hot. Drain the pasta well, and divide between 2 dishes. Spoon over the hot sauce.

Pasta 'n bean bake ◉
Serves 4

175 g/6 oz Record whole wheat pasta rings
300 ml/½ pint milk
300 ml/½ pint packet cheese sauce mix
2 tablespoons oil
1 medium onion, chopped
425 g/15 oz can baked beans
2 tablespoons tomato ketchup
25 g/1 oz cheese, grated

Cook the pasta and drain well in a colander. Meanwhile, pour the milk into a small saucepan, sprinkle in the cheese sauce mix and whisk over moderate heat until the sauce comes to the boil. Remove from the heat. Put the oil and onion into the pan used for cooking the pasta and place over moderate heat until the onion is soft but not brown. Stir in the baked beans and ketchup with a tablespoon and remove from the heat.

Grease an ovenproof pie dish and put in half the pasta to make an even layer. Spoon over half the baked bean mixture, then cover with half the cheese sauce. Make another three layers like this – pasta, baked bean mixture and cheese sauce. Sprinkle with the cheese. Stand the pie dish on a baking sheet and place in a moderately hot oven (200°C/400°F/Gas Mark 6) for 20 minutes. Serve with a green salad.

Pasta 'n bean bake

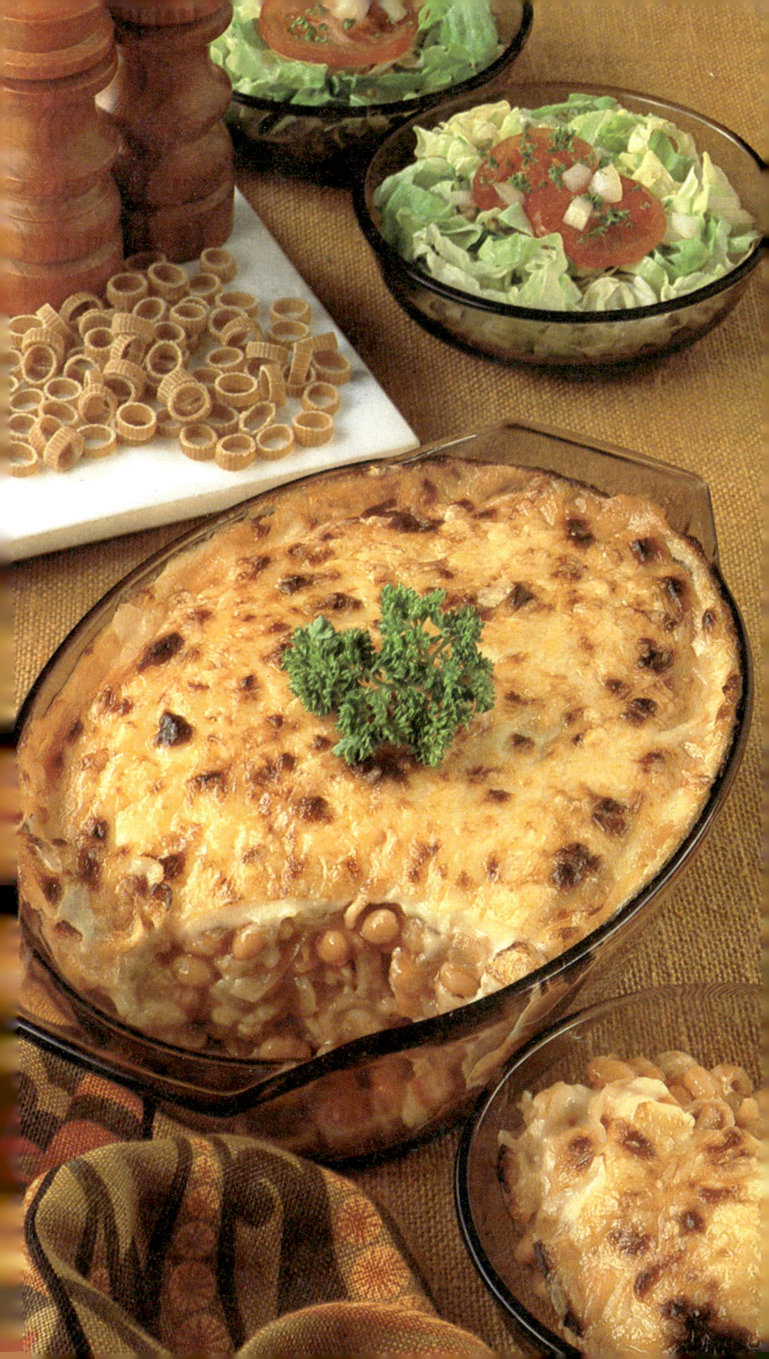

Sardines in hiding
Serves 4

2 × 100 g/4 oz cans sardines in tomato sauce
300 ml/½ pint packet savoury white sauce mix
300 ml/½ pint milk
175 g/6 oz Record pasta shells, cooked
2 eggs, separated
salt and pepper

Arrange the sardines and tomato sauce in the base of an ovenproof dish. Place the sauce mix and milk in a saucepan and whisk until the sauce is boiling. Remove from the heat and stir in the pasta and egg yolks. Taste and add salt and pepper if necessary. Whip the egg whites until stiff and fold into the pasta mixture just until well combined, then spoon over the sardines in the dish. Bake in a moderate oven (180°C/350°F/Gas Mark 4) for 40–45 minutes, until golden brown on top.

Mandarin magic
Serves 4

311 g/11 oz can mandarin oranges
75 g/3 oz Record short-cut macaroni, cooked
1 small can condensed milk
2 tablespoons lemon juice
8 currants

Drain the mandarins, reserving the syrup and 4 neat segments, and mix the remainder with the pasta. Divide between 4 round serving dishes and press lightly to flatten. Place the condensed milk in a bowl and stir in the lemon juice and 2 tablespoons of the reserved syrup. The mixture will thicken slightly, then spoon it into the dishes over the pasta mixture. Decorate each dessert to make a smiling face, using a reserved mandarin segment for the mouth and currants for the eyes.

Chocolate brittle

Makes about 70 squares

50 g/2 oz butter *or* margarine
2 tablespoons golden syrup
2 tablespoons cocoa powder
4 tablespoons castor sugar
50 g/2 oz Record Durum wheat bran

Place the butter or margarine and golden syrup in a large saucepan and stir with a wooden spoon over gentle heat until the fat has melted. Add the cocoa and sugar and stir well until the mixture is smooth. Remove the pan from the heat and stir in the bran. Spread this mixture in a greased Swiss roll tin and place in a moderate oven (180°C/350°F/Gas Mark 4) for 8 minutes. Remove the tin from the oven and mark the mixture into 2.5 cm/1 in. squares with a knife. Leave until cold, then break the brittle into pieces. Store in an airtight container.

CHAPTER 2

SLIMMING SUCCESSFULLY WITH PASTA

An important aspect of any good slimming diet is the variety and attractiveness of the food permitted. Of course, vegetables and fruit are essential, and many would-be dieters find it hard to include as many foods in this category as they should. A fresh fruit breakfast is ideal – try sliced oranges, grapefruit or banana sprinkled with Record Durum wheat bran. Sometimes a delicate and delicious soup can make quite a satisfying meal, especially for the light meal of the day, whether it is lunch or supper. These recipes omit any kind of starchy thickening agent and spend calories wisely on a proportion of highly-nutritious pasta. This section also includes really unusual hot main dishes and super, exciting salads – all calorie counted to suit a weight-watcher's needs.

Light Soups

Chopped chicken and prawn soup ❺
Serves 4
Each portion=approx. 120 calories

100 g/4 oz portion boneless chicken breast
1 litre/1¾ pints chicken stock
50 g/2 oz Record vermicelli
50 g/2 oz shelled prawns, chopped
salt and pepper
chopped chives

Place the chicken breast in a saucepan with the stock and bring slowly to the boil. Skim if necessary, cover and simmer for 20 minutes. Lift out the chicken breast. Crumble the pasta into the stock, bring to the boil again and cook for 4–6 minutes, or until the pasta is tender. Meanwhile, cut the chicken into strips. Stir the chicken strips and prawns into the soup, bring back to boiling point again and add salt and pepper to taste. Serve hot sprinkled with chives.

Egg and lemon soup ◐
Serves 4
Each portion=approx. 100 calories

1 litre/1¾ pints chicken stock
50 g/2 oz Record soup pasta shells
salt and pepper
2 eggs, separated
juice of 1 lemon

Place the stock in a large saucepan and bring to the boil. Stir in the pasta and cook for about 10 minutes, or until the pasta is tender. Season to taste with salt and pepper. Place the egg whites in a bowl and whisk until stiff. Add the egg yolks and whisk until the mixture is creamy. Keep whisking and gradually add the lemon juice and about one third of the hot stock. Pour the egg mixture into the remaining hot stock, whisking constantly over gentle heat for 1 minute. Adjust the seasoning if necessary and serve immediately.

Lettuce and pea soup **F**
Serves 4
Each portion=approx. 90 calories

1 litre/1¾ pints water
1 chicken stock cube
1 medium onion, sliced
1 small lettuce, shredded
100 g/4 oz frozen minted peas
2 teaspoons lemon juice
salt and pepper
2 tablespoons dried low fat milk powder
50 g/2 oz Record short-cut macaroni, cooked
1 tablespoon chopped mint

Place the water in a saucepan, crumble in the stock cube and bring to the boil. Add the onion, lettuce, peas and lemon juice. Bring back to the boil, add salt and pepper to taste, cover and simmer for 20 minutes. Liquidise the soup, return to the rinsed pan and sprinkle in the milk powder. Stir well, add the pasta and reheat thoroughly. Adjust the seasoning if necessary and serve sprinkled with mint.

Note If minted peas are not available, add ¼ teaspoon concentrated mint sauce with the vegetables.

Beetroot soup with dill

Serves 4
Each portion=approx. 130 calories

1 large raw beetroot (about 350 g/12 oz)
2 teaspoons oil
1 litre/1¾ pints hot beef stock
salt and pepper
50 g/2 oz Record quick-cook macaroni
4 tablespoons natural yogurt
½ teaspoon dried dill weed

Peel the beetroot thinly, then grate it. Heat the oil in a thick-bottomed pan, reserve 1 tablespoon of the grated beetroot and add the rest to the pan. Stir over moderate heat until it begins to soften. Add the stock, bring to the boil and season to taste. Cover and simmer for about 20 minutes, or until the beetroot is soft. Strain the soup and return to the rinsed pan. Bring to the boil, add the pasta and cook for 6–8 minutes, or until the pasta is tender. Tie the reserved raw beetroot in a square of muslin and add to the soup to restore the bright colour. Reheat to boiling point, taste and adjust the seasoning if necessary, then remove the bag of beetroot. Serve hot, with a tablespoon of yogurt swirled into each portion and dill sprinkled on top.

Super Salads

Cucumber drum salad
Serves 4
Each portion=approx. 280 calories

1 large cucumber
1 sweet red pepper
200 g/7 oz can tuna
juice of 1 small orange
1 tablespoon low calorie salad dressing
½ teaspoon French mustard
100 g/4 oz Record pasta wheels, cooked

Cut stripes of skin away from the cucumber with a canell or pointed knife. Cut the cucumber into 5 cm/2 in. lengths and scoop out the centres. Reserve the cucumber flesh, leaving drum-shaped cases. Deseed the pepper and cut it into fine strips. Drain and flake the tuna, using the oil and juices to make a dressing with the orange juice, salad dressing and mustard, beating it well. Chop the reserved cucumber and half the pepper strips, keeping back the best ones for the garnish. Combine the pasta, chopped cucumber, pepper and the tuna. Arrange the cucumber drums on a serving platter. Pile up the filling inside them and pour over a little dressing. Arrange pepper strips at each end of the dish.

Cucumber drum salad

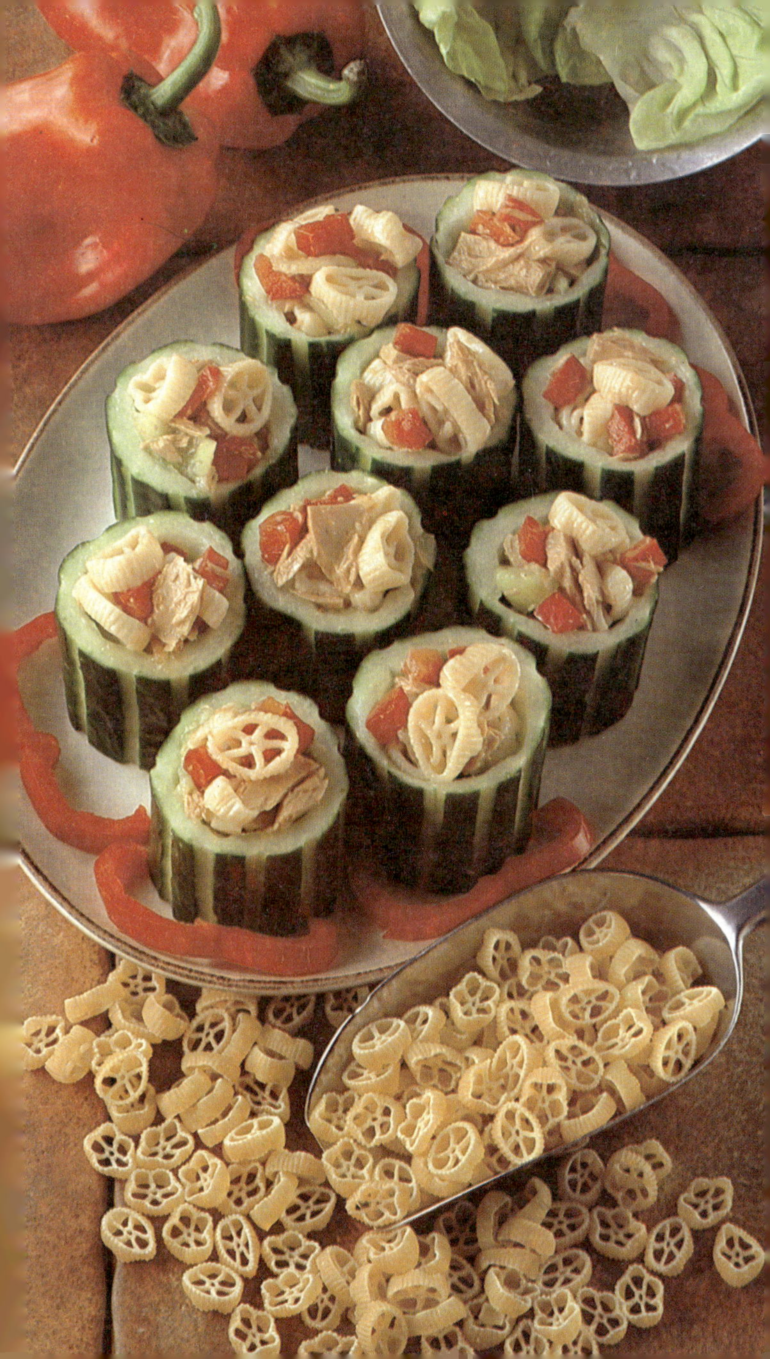

Frankfurter summer salad ⓠ

Serves 4
Each portion=approx. 310 calories

350 g/12 oz frankfurter sausages
175 g/6 oz Record pasta twistetti, cooked
100 g/4 oz cooked French beans
3 medium tomatoes, chopped
1 small sweet green pepper, deseeded
shredded lettuce
8 stuffed green olives, sliced
Dressing
1 tablespoon low calorie salad dressing
1 tablespoon mild continental mustard
150 ml/¼ pint natural yogurt

First make the dressing by blending the three ingredients together. Cut the frankfurters into thick diagonal slices and combine with the pasta, beans and chopped tomato. Cut the pepper into large dice and add to the salad with the dressing. Toss lightly until coated and chill for about 1 hour. Serve on a bed of shredded lettuce and sprinkle the olives over the top.

Pasta and garlic sausage salad ⓠ

Serves 4
Each portion=approx. 475 calories

175 g/6 oz Record pasta shells
150 ml/¼ pint French dressing
4 large spring onions, trimmed
2 red-skinned dessert apples, cored
2 tablespoons lemon juice
225 g/8 oz piece of garlic sausage, diced
salt and black pepper
1 small onion
3 tablespoons chopped fresh parsley

Cook the pasta, drain well and turn into a bowl. Stir in just sufficient dressing to coat the pasta and allow to cool, stirring occasionally. Chop the spring onions and the apples and mix with the lemon juice. Add to the pasta with the garlic sausage. Add seasoning to taste. Cover and chill for about 1 hour. Finely chop the onion and stir into the remaining dressing with the parsley. Serve separately with the salad.

Herbed chicken salad
Serves 4
Each portion=approx. 500 calories

100 g/4 oz fresh spinach leaves, washed
4 tablespoons mayonnaise
150 ml/¼ pint natural yogurt
1 ripe avocado
2 tablespoons lemon juice
salt and pepper
175 g/6 oz Record pasta spirals, cooked
225 g/8 oz cooked chicken, diced
1 tablespoon chopped parsley
1 tablespoon chopped mint
1 tablespoon chopped chives

Cook 2 large leaves of spinach in the water clinging to the leaves in a small covered pan, until limp. Press liquid out through a sieve and use to colour the mayonnaise. Stir in the yogurt. Halve, stone and peel the avocado. Dice one half and slice the other half. Sprinkle with the lemon juice. Allow to stand for 5 minutes, then drain the juices into the mayonnaise. Season to taste. Mix together the pasta, chicken, herbs, diced avocado and mayonnaise. Shred the remaining spinach leaves and use to line a salad bowl. Pile up the chicken mixture in the centre and garnish with the avocado slices.

Edam and grape platter

Serves 4
Each portion=approx. 400 calories

225 g/8 oz black grapes, halved
175 g/6 oz Record twistetti, cooked
175 g/6 oz frankfurter sausages, sliced
100 g/4 oz Edam cheese, cubed
shredded lettuce
chopped fennel
fennel leaves
Dressing
4 tablespoons natural yogurt
1 tablespoon lemon juice
finely grated rind of 1 lemon
salt and black pepper

Remove the pips from the grapes and combine them with the pasta, frankfurters and cheese. Beat together the yogurt, lemon juice, lemon rind and seasoning to taste to make a dressing. Pour over the cheese mixture and toss lightly. Make a bed of lettuce and fennel on a serving platter and arrange the cheese salad on top. Serve garnished with fennel leaves.

Edam and grape platter

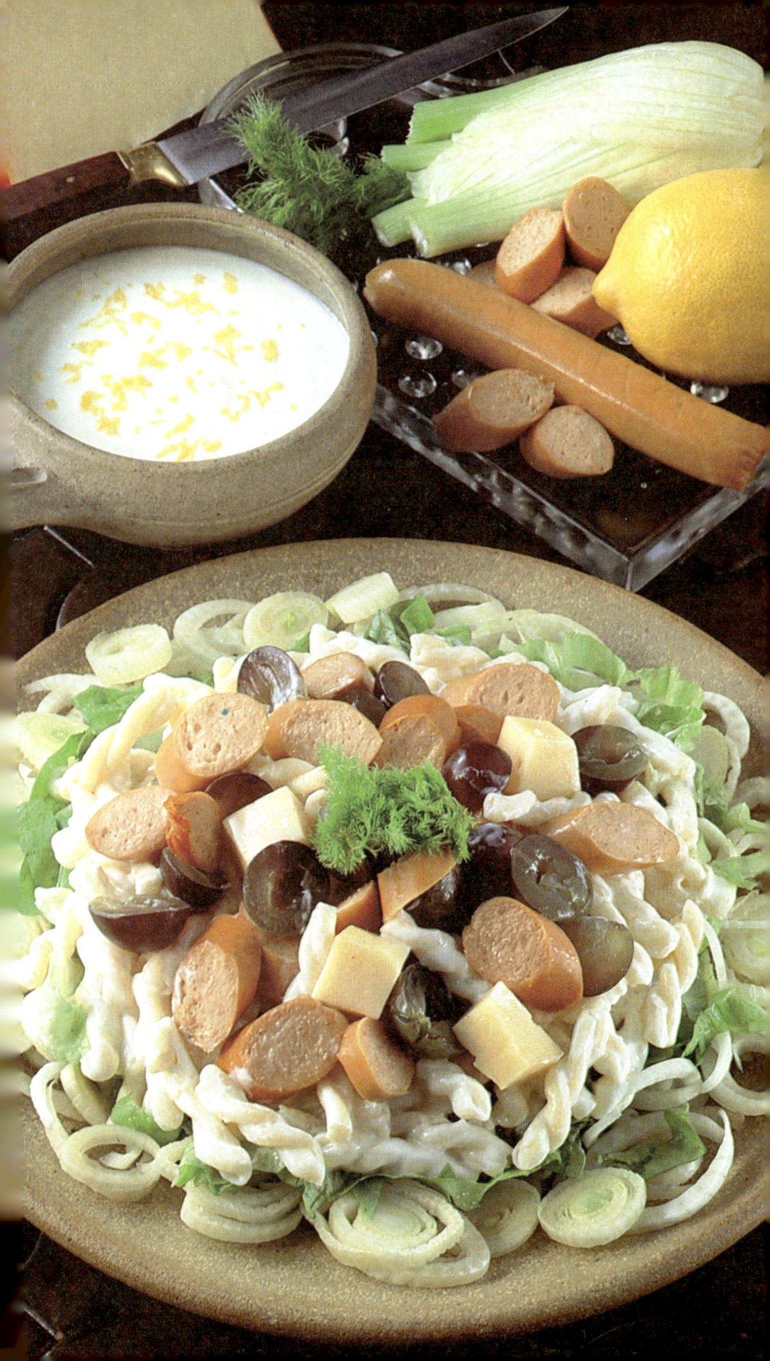

Low Calorie Dishes

Fennel and ham gratin
Serves 4
Each portion=approx. 280 calories

100 g/4 oz lean ham
4 small *or* 2 large heads of fennel
75 g/3 oz Record pasta caramelle
1 tablespoon oil
1 medium onion, chopped
396 g/14 oz can tomatoes
1 tablespoon tomato purée
2 bay leaves
salt and pepper
50 g/2 oz Cheddar cheese, grated

Cut the ham into strips. Trim the fennel and cut in halves or quarters, depending on size. Cook in boiling, salted water for about 15 minutes, or until just tender. Meanwhile, cook the pasta, drain well and mix with the ham. Place in a shallow heatproof dish. Drain the fennel, reserving 4 tablespoons of the cooking liquid, and arrange on the pasta mixture. Keep hot.

Place the oil in the pan used for cooking the pasta and use to fry the onion gently until soft. Roughly chop the tomatoes and add to the pan with the liquid from the can, the tomato purée, bay leaves and reserved liquid. Bring to the boil and stir over moderate heat for 2 minutes. Remove the bay leaves, season with salt and pepper and pour over the fennel. Sprinkle with the cheese and grill until golden brown on top.

Fish in spinach sauce

Serves 4
Each portion=approx. 250 calories

450 g/1 lb fillets of whiting *or* lemon sole
salt and pepper
300 ml/½ pint milk
75 g/3 oz Record short-cut macaroni
225 g/8 oz frozen chopped spinach, defrosted
1 teaspoon cornflour
grated rind and juice of ½ lemon
½ teaspoon ground nutmeg
4 lemon slices

Arrange the fish fillets in a shallow oval ovenproof dish, sprinkle with salt and pepper and pour over the milk. Cover and cook in a moderately hot oven (190°C/375°F/Gas Mark 5) for 15 minutes. Meanwhile, cook the pasta. Remove the fish from the oven and drain the cooking liquid into a saucepan. Drain the pasta, spoon it around the fish fillets in the dish. Cover the dish again and return it to the oven while you make the sauce.

Add the spinach to the milk liquid and stir until boiling. Moisten the cornflour with the lemon juice and add to the pan, stirring constantly until the sauce is smooth and thick. Mix in the lemon rind and nutmeg and season to taste with salt and pepper. Simmer for 2 minutes. Pour the spinach sauce over the pasta and garnish the fish fillets with lemon slices. Serve at once.

Cottage cheese omelette

Serves 2
Each portion=approx. 350 calories

1 large rasher streaky bacon, chopped
3 spring onions, chopped
4 eggs
75 g/3 oz cottage cheese
50 g/2 oz cooked Record quick-cook macaroni
salt and pepper

Place the bacon in a small frying pan and heat slowly until the fat begins to run. Raise the heat and fry until the bacon bits are golden and crisp. Add the onion and fry for 2 minutes. Beat the eggs with the cottage cheese and stir in the pasta. Season with salt and pepper and pour into the pan. Stir with a fork over moderate heat, until the mixture is almost cooked, then spread flat in the pan and cook on until the underneath is golden brown and the top set. Fold over and slide on to a warm plate.

Note The small quantity of pasta required for this recipe makes it a perfect choice when a little is left over from a previous meal.

Cottage cheese omelette

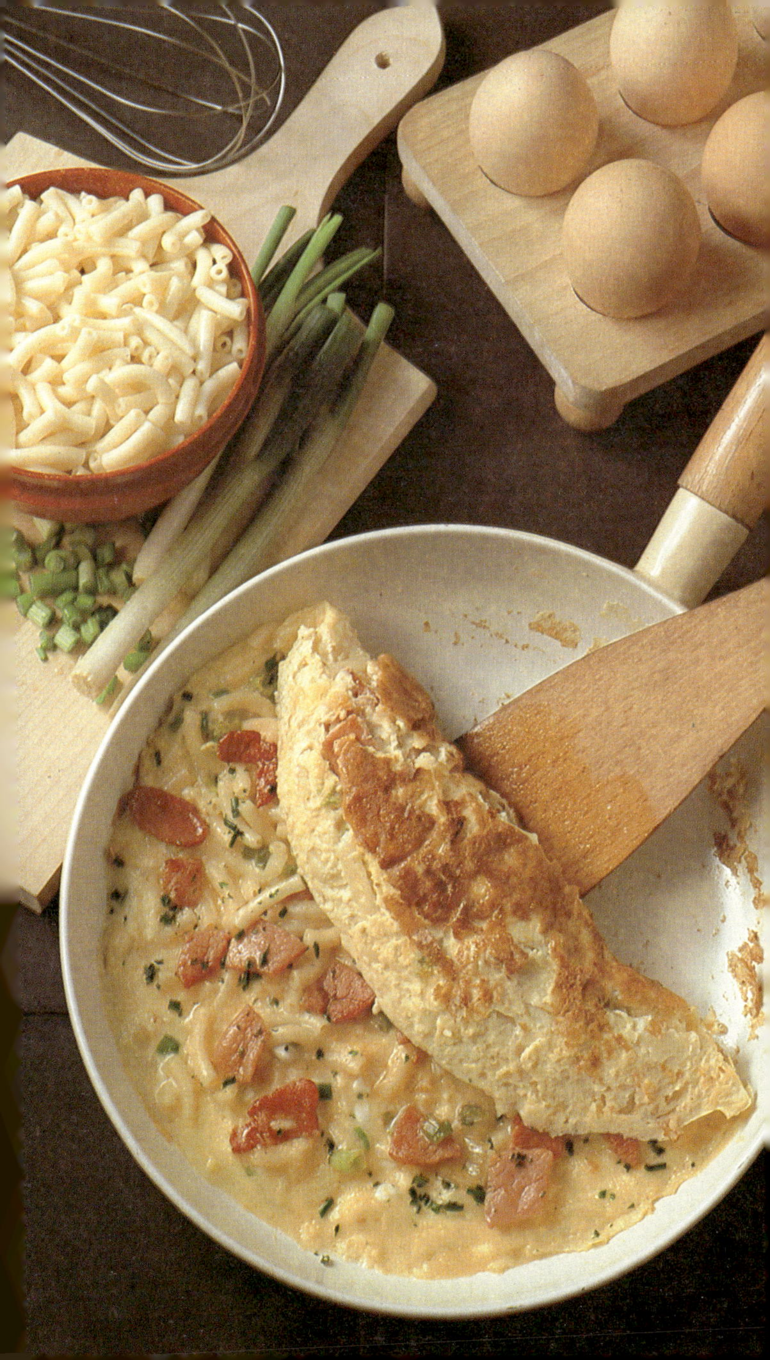

Baked chicken custard
Serves 4
Each portion=approx. 300 calories

225 g/8 oz pack frozen mixed vegetables
175 g/6 oz cooked chicken, chopped
75 g/3 oz Record soup pasta shells, cooked
3 eggs, separated
300 ml/½ pint milk
½ teaspoon dry mustard
salt and pepper
tomato wedges

Cook the vegetables in a little boiling, salted water until tender. Drain well, mix with the chicken and pasta and spoon evenly into a well-greased flan dish. Beat the eggs with the milk and mustard and season generously with salt and pepper. Pour carefully over the chicken mixture in the dish. Bake in a moderately hot oven (190°C/375°F/Gas Mark 5) for about 30 minutes, or until the custard is firm and golden brown on top. Serve garnished with tomato wedges.

CHAPTER 3

FULL~VALUE VEGETARIAN DISHES

With such increasing interest in vegetarian eating, many more people are prepared to enjoy a meal without meat. There is certainly no need to be limited to the boring nut cutlet. New horizons open up when you cook vegetarian food using such ingredients as nutty brown whole wheat pasta, peanut butter, roasted sunflower seeds and exotic vegetables such as aubergines and courgettes. All the dishes in this section are packed with protein to provide well-balanced meals for maximum energy.

Peanut pasta burgers
Serves 4

50 ml/2 fl oz oil
50 g/2 oz plain flour
300 ml/½ pint water
1 teaspoon yeast extract spread
1 teaspoon tomato purée
75 g/3 oz salted peanuts, chopped
75 g/3 oz Record whole wheat short-cut macaroni, cooked
1 egg
1 tablespoon water
100 g/4 oz fresh breadcrumbs
oil for frying
lettuce leaves
tomato wedges
green pepper strips

Place the oil in a saucepan and blend in the flour. Gradually add the water and bring to the boil, stirring all the time, until the mixture bubbles. It should be smooth and very thick. Cook gently for 2 minutes, stirring constantly. Remove from the heat and mix in the yeast extract spread, tomato purée, peanuts and pasta. Divide the mixture into 8 equal portions and shape each into a round flat cake with floured hands. Beat the egg with the water. Dip the burgers in the egg mixture, then coat all over with breadcrumbs. Shallow fry in oil for about 3 minutes on each side, until golden brown. Drain well. Arrange a bed of lettuce leaves on a serving dish, place the hot burgers on top and garnish with tomato wedges and pepper strips.

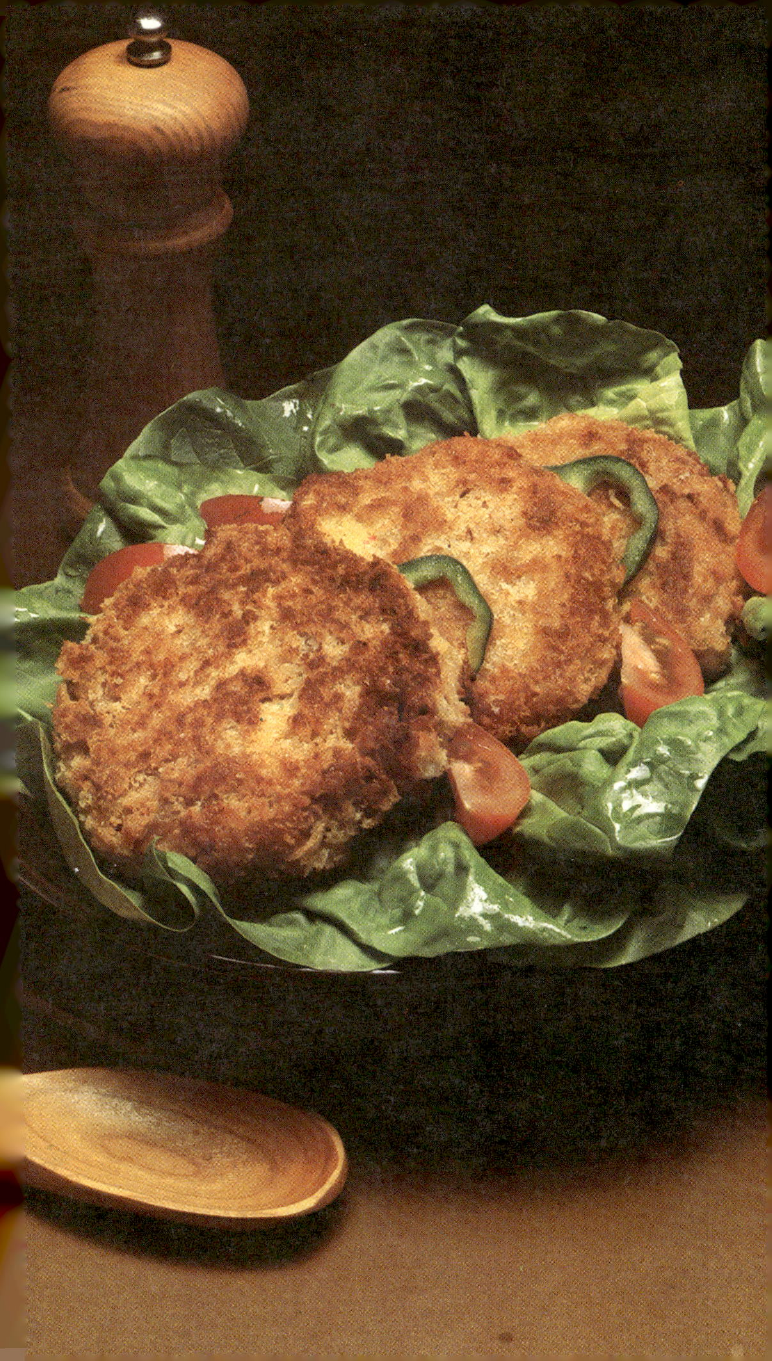

Vegetable fritters with lemon sauce
Serves 4

1 medium aubergine (about 225 g/8 oz)
225 g/8 oz courgettes
salt
175 g/6 oz Record whole wheat spaghetti
50 g/2 oz cream cheese
75 g/3 oz plain flour
2 tablespoons Record Durum wheat bran
2 eggs
1 teaspoon sweet paprika pepper
4 tablespoons water
oil for frying
Sauce
25 g/1 oz butter *or* margarine
20 g/¾ oz plain flour
300 ml/½ pint milk
finely-grated rind of 1 lemon
pinch of sugar
2–3 tablespoons lemon juice
salt and pepper

Cut the aubergine into thick slices and divide these in half if large. Cut the courgettes into 2 cm/¾ in. slices. Sprinkle the vegetables with salt and allow to stand for 10 minutes. Meanwhile, cook the pasta and make the batter. Soften the cream cheese and gradually blend in the flour, bran, eggs, paprika and water to make a thick batter.

To make the sauce, place the butter or margarine, flour and milk in a saucepan and whisk until the sauce boils and thickens. Blend in the lemon rind and sugar and add lemon juice and seasoning to taste. The sauce should be strongly flavoured with lemon but not bitter. Simmer for 5 minutes and keep hot while you fry the fritters.

Rinse the vegetable pieces and dry really well on soft kitchen paper. Dip pieces of courgette and aubergine in the batter and deep fry, a few at a time, in moderately hot oil (170°C/340°F) for about 3–4 minutes, or until crisp and brown. Do not have the oil too hot or the batter will brown before the vegetable centres are tender. Drain well and keep hot. Drain the pasta and place in a hot serving dish. Arrange the fritters on top and pour over the lemon sauce.

Curried egg caramelle   Ⓠ
Serves 4

225 g/8 oz Record pasta caramelle
4 eggs
salt and pepper
3 tablespoons oil
2 medium onions, sliced
2 cloves garlic, crushed
100 g/4 oz button mushrooms, sliced
2 teaspoons curry powder
1 teaspoon ground turmeric
100 g/4 oz hot cooked green peas

Cook the pasta. Meanwhile, beat 2 eggs and season well. Brush a large frying pan with a little of the oil, pour in the beaten egg and make a thin omelette. When set, turn out on a plate and make another omelette in the same way using the remaining eggs. Place the second omelette on top of the first and cut them into narrow strips. Keep the longer strips for the garnish and snip up the remainder. Keep warm.

Place the rest of the oil in a saucepan and use to fry the onion and garlic gently until soft. Add the mushrooms and fry until they are soft. Stir in the curry powder and turmeric and fry, stirring, for a further 3 minutes. Drain the pasta well, add it to the curry mixture and stir until coated. Fold in the hot peas and chopped omelettes and add seasoning to taste. Serve on a warm platter, garnished with a latticework of reserved omelette strips.

Macaroni and aubergine pie
Serves 6

350 g/12 oz puff pastry
175 g/6 oz Record short-cut macaroni
1 large aubergine (about 350 g/12 oz)
oil
2 eggs, hard-boiled
50 g/2 oz margarine
40 g/1½ oz plain flour
450 ml/¾ pint milk
salt and black pepper
100 g/4 oz Cheddar cheese, grated

Roll out the pastry thinly and use to line a shallow oblong ovenproof dish. Pull up the sides of the pastry and pinch to make a firm edge. Prick the base and chill until required.

Cook the pasta. Meanwhile, thinly slice the aubergine and brush each slice generously with oil on both sides. Arrange the slices in a single layer on a baking sheet and place in a moderately hot oven (190°C/375°F/Gas Mark 5) for 8 minutes. Drain the pasta well and chop the eggs.

Place the margarine, flour and milk in a saucepan and whisk over moderate heat until the sauce boils and thickens. Stir in the pasta, chopped egg and seasoning to taste. Add half the cheese and spoon this mixture evenly into the pastry case. Arrange overlapping aubergine slices on top and sprinkle with the rest of the cheese. Cover lightly with foil and bake in the oven for 30 minutes. Remove the foil and continue baking for a further 10 minutes. Serve hot.

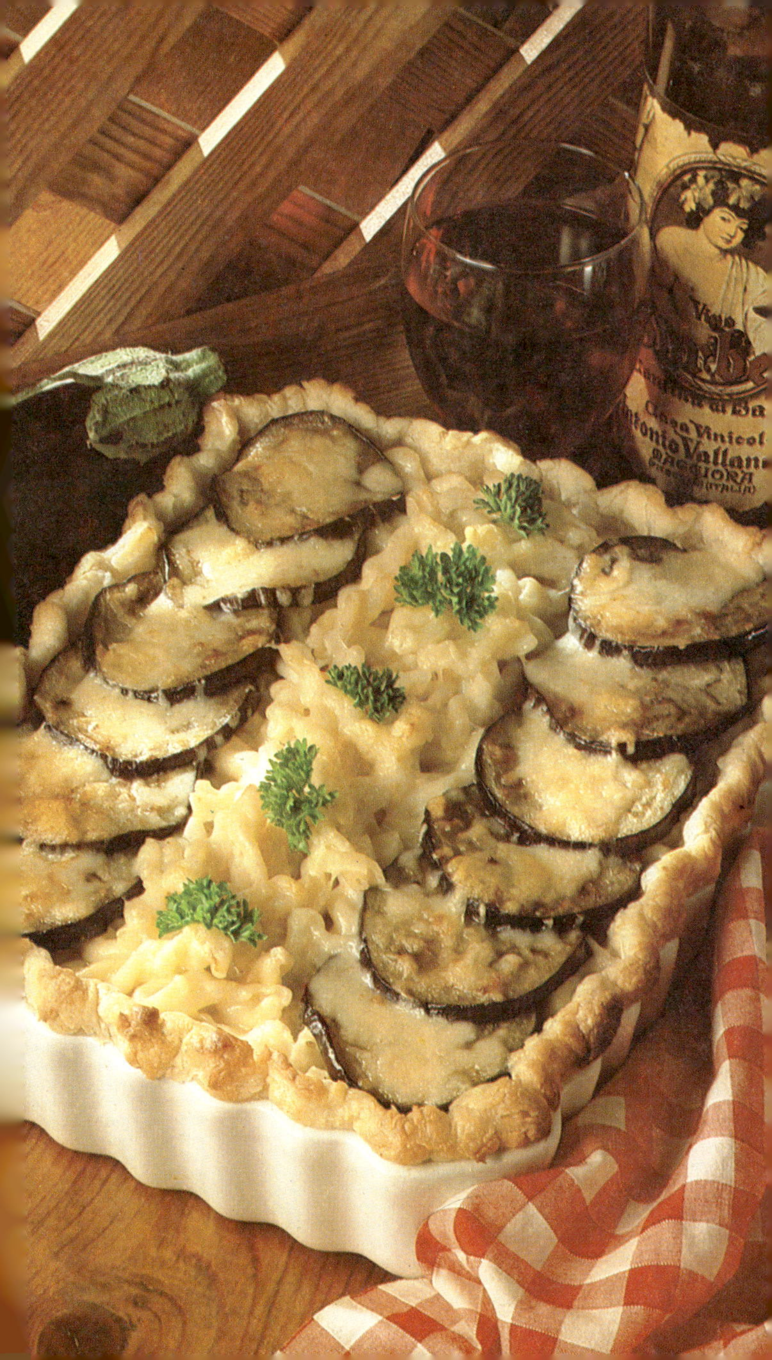

Vegetarian lasagne verdi
Serves 4

2 tablespoons oil
225 g/8 oz leeks, sliced
225 g/8 oz celery, chopped
100 g/4 oz parsnips, sliced
225 g/8 oz can tomatoes
1 teaspoon dried mixed herbs
1 tablespoon tomato purée
1 teaspoon sugar
1 teaspoon soy sauce
50 g/2 oz stuffed green olives, sliced
salt and black pepper
40 g/1½ oz margarine
25 g/1 oz plain flour
300 ml/½ pint milk
150 g/5 oz Cheddar cheese, grated
175 g/6 oz Record lasagne verdi, cooked
100 g/4 oz cottage cheese

Heat the oil and use to fry the leeks, celery and parsnips until the leeks start to soften. Add the tomatoes and liquid from the can, the herbs, tomato purée, sugar and soy sauce. Bring to the boil, stirring, then cook gently for 30 minutes. Stir in the olives and season the sauce with salt and pepper. Place the margarine, flour and milk in a saucepan and whisk over moderate heat until the sauce boils and thickens. Stir in most of the grated cheese and as soon as the sauce is smooth again, remove from the heat and season to taste.

Grease an oblong ovenproof dish and put one-third of the lasagne as a layer in the bottom. Cover with half the tomato mixture, then spoon over half the cottage cheese. Repeat these layers once, top with the remaining lasagne and pour over the cheese sauce. Sprinkle with the rest of the cheese and bake in a moderately hot oven (200°C/400°F/Gas Mark 6) for 25 minutes, until golden brown on top.

Spaghetti with lentil sauce ⓠ
Serves 4

100 g/4 oz lentils
2 tablespoons oil
1 large onion, chopped
396 g/14 oz can tomatoes
2 tablespoons tomato purée
25 g/1 oz chopped walnuts
1 vegetable stock cube
1 tablespoon cornflour
salt and pepper
225 g/8 oz Record whole wheat spaghetti

Soak the lentils in cold water for 2 hours. Drain well. Heat half the oil and use to fry the onion until soft. Reserve 2 tablespoons liquid from the can of tomatoes and add the rest to the onion with the tomatoes, tomato purée, lentils, nuts and crumbled stock cube. Bring to the boil, cover and simmer for 15 minutes.

Blend together the reserved liquid and the cornflour, add to the lentil sauce and bring back to the boil, stirring constantly. Simmer for 2 minutes and season to taste. Meanwhile, cook the pasta, drain well and stir in the remaining oil to coat the strands. Serve on a warm dish with the lentil sauce poured over.

Hot cheesey squares ⓕ
Serves 4

600 ml/1 pint milk
1 small onion, sliced
1 bay leaf
100 g/4 oz Record whole wheat semolina
175 g/6 oz Cheddar cheese, grated
20 g/¾ oz margarine
1 teaspoon made English mustard
salt and pepper

Place the milk in a saucepan and bring to boiling point. Put the onion and bay leaf in a bowl, pour over the milk, cover and allow to stand until cool. Strain the flavoured milk back into the saucepan and bring to the boil. Sprinkle on the semolina and boil, stirring constantly, for 5 minutes. Remove the pan from the heat and stir in half the cheese, the margarine and mustard. Season to taste with salt and pepper and spread the mixture in a flat dish to a depth of about 2 cm/¾ in. Allow to cool. When the mixture is cold and firm cut it into squares and arrange these in a greased shallow ovenproof dish. Sprinkle with the rest of the cheese and cook in a moderately hot oven (200°C/400°F/Gas Mark 6) for 20 minutes, or until golden brown.

Blushing beetroot salad
Serves 4

311 g/11 oz can mandarin oranges in natural juice
1 tablespoon vinegar
225 g/8 oz cooked beetroot, diced
50 g/2 oz cottage cheese, sieved
1 tablespoon peanut butter
100 g/4 oz Record spaghetti rings, cooked
100 g/4 oz Lancashire *or* Caerphilly cheese, diced
salt and pepper
few onion rings

Drain the oranges and use 2 tablespoons of the juice, with the vinegar, to pour over the beetroot. Allow to stand for 30 minutes. Drain the liquid into the cottage cheese, add the peanut butter and beat well until blended. Combine the pasta, cheese, orange segments and beetroot and fold in the pink dressing. Add salt and pepper if necessary. Divide the salad between 4 large wine glasses and garnish each serving with raw onion rings.

Blushing beetroot salad

Apricot and cucumber salad
Serves 4

grated rind and juice of 1 lemon
1 tablespoon clear honey
150 ml/¼ pint natural yogurt
salt and pepper
1 medium mild onion
1 large cucumber
100 g/4 oz dried apricots
175 g/6 oz Record pasta spirals, cooked
50 g/2 oz pine *or* cashew nuts
lettuce leaves
2 tablespoons chopped mixed fresh herbs (parsley, chives, mint, marjoram)

Beat the lemon rind and juice and the honey into the yogurt. Season to taste with salt and pepper. Slice the onion and divide into rings. Dice the cucumber and cut the apricots into strips. Combine the onion, cucumber, apricot, pasta and nuts. Pour over the dressing and toss lightly until coated. Arrange a bed of lettuce leaves on a serving platter, top with the salad mixture and sprinkle with the herbs.

Pasta beignets with sunrise sauce
Serves 4

100 g/4 oz plain flour
½ teaspoon salt
pinch of pepper
¼ teaspoon dry mustard
150 ml/¼ pint lukewarm water
1 tablespoon oil
100 g/4 oz Record whole wheat short-cut macaroni, cooked
2 egg whites
oil for frying
Sauce
298 g/10½ oz can condensed cream of tomato soup
¼ teaspoon ground ginger
grated rind and juice of 2 oranges
salt and pepper

First make the sauce. Turn the soup into a small saucepan and blend in the ginger and orange rind and juice. Stir until boiling and add extra seasoning if wished. Keep the sauce hot while you make the beignets.

Sift the flour, salt, pepper and mustard into a bowl and add the water and oil. Whisk well until smooth. Stir in the pasta. Whisk the egg whites until stiff and fold into the pasta mixture. Shallow fry the beignets a few at a time, in oil over moderate heat, using a good tablespoon of the mixture for each one, for 4–6 minutes turning once, until crisp and golden brown on both sides. Drain well and serve hot with the sauce.

Leek and cheese special **F**
Serves 4

4 medium leeks
175 g/6 oz Record whole wheat spaghetti rings
25 g/1 oz butter *or* margarine
1 medium onion, chopped
175 g/6 oz button mushrooms, sliced
Sauce
25 g/1 oz butter *or* margarine
2 tablespoons flour
450 ml/¾ pint milk
150 g/5 oz Cheddar cheese, grated
pinch of ground nutmeg
salt and pepper

Trim the roots from the leeks and cut each one to a length of 15 cm/6 in., removing and reserving the green tops. Split each leek in half lengthways and wash well. Cook with the pasta in plenty of boiling salted water for about 15 minutes, or until just tender. Meanwhile, finely chop the reserved leek tops. Melt the butter and use to cook the onion and chopped leek until golden. Add the mushrooms and fry, stirring, for a further 3 minutes. Keep hot while you make the sauce.

Place the butter, flour and milk in a small saucepan and whisk over moderate heat until the sauce boils and thickens. Simmer for 2 minutes. Stir in most of the cheese, the nutmeg and seasoning to taste. As soon as the sauce is smooth, remove from the heat and stir in the onion, leek and mushroom mixture.

When the leeks and pasta are tender, drain well and place in a shallow ovenproof dish. Pour over the cheese sauce mixture and sprinkle with the remaining cheese. Place under a hot grill for a few minutes, until golden brown and bubbling.

Cauliflower with peanut butter pasta ◉
Serves 4

1 medium cauliflower
100 g/4 oz Record pasta wheels
50 g/2 oz butter *or* margarine
1 medium onion, chopped
2 sticks celery, chopped
25 g/1 oz plain flour
750 ml/1¼ pints milk
salt and pepper
100 g/4 oz crunchy peanut butter

Divide the cauliflower into florets. Cook in boiling salted water for about 10 minutes, until tender. Meanwhile, cook the pasta and make the sauce. Melt the butter or margarine in a large saucepan and use to fry the onion and celery gently until the celery is tender. Sprinkle over the flour and stir until well blended. Cook for 1 minute, then gradually add the milk and bring to the boil, stirring constantly. Simmer for 4 minutes and season generously with salt and pepper to taste.

Drain the cauliflower and place in a hot shallow serving dish. Stir the peanut butter into the sauce until evenly mixed, then drain the pasta and fold into the sauce. Pour the pasta mixture over the cauliflower and serve at once.

CHAPTER 4

INSPIRED PASTA PUDDINGS

Original ideas for sweet dishes to make a change from roly-poly and rice pudding are always in demand. These recipes for puddings and desserts are deliciously different; even the titles show how far we have departed from the humdrum. They will make welcome newcomers to family meals, and many of them are exciting enough to win compliments from guests.

Everyday Puddings and Desserts

Orange butterscotch shells
Serves 4

450 ml/¾ pint milk
75 g/3 oz Record pasta shells
finely-grated rind of 2 oranges
40 g/1½ oz castor sugar
Sauce
juice of 2 oranges
50 g/2 oz butter *or* margarine
75 g/3 oz soft brown sugar
4 teaspoons cornflour
2 tablespoons cold water
pinch of salt

Place the milk, pasta and orange rind in a heavy saucepan and bring to the boil, stirring. Cover and simmer for about 20 minutes, stirring frequently, until the pasta is tender and the mixture thickened.

Meanwhile, make the sauce. Make up the orange juice to 225 ml/7 fl oz with water and heat to boiling point. Place the butter or margarine and sugar in a small pan and heat gently until melted. Stir in the hot liquid until the mixture is well combined. Moisten the cornflour with the cold water, add to the pan and bring to the boil, stirring constantly, until the sauce thickens. Stir in the salt.

Mix the castor sugar with the pasta and turn into an ovenproof dish. Carefully pour over the sauce and bake in a moderately hot oven (190°C/375°F/Gas Mark 5) for 20 minutes.

Prune and pasta delight
Serves 4

225 g/8 oz dried prunes
about 450 ml/¾ pint cold tea
about 3 tablespoons soft brown sugar
75 g/3 oz Record whole wheat spaghetti rings, cooked

Place the prunes in a saucepan and pour over sufficient tea to cover. Allow to soak overnight. Add 2 tablespoons sugar and bring to the boil. Cover and simmer for about 10 minutes, until the prunes are tender. Lift them out of the syrup, stone if desired, and mix with the pasta. Place in a glass dish. Taste the syrup, add a little more sugar if wished and stir until dissolved. Reduce slightly by boiling until syrupy, then spoon over the pasta and prunes and chill well.

Ring puffs with cherry sauce
Serves 4–6

100 g/4 oz butter *or* margarine
300 ml/½ pint water
150 g/5 oz plain flour
3 eggs, separated
75 g/3 oz Record spaghetti rings, cooked
oil for frying
little castor sugar
Sauce
297 g/10½ oz can cherry pie filling
4 tablespoons orange juice
2 tablespoons cherry brandy *or* sherry
little castor sugar

First make the sauce. Turn the pie filling into a small saucepan and blend in the orange juice and brandy. Bring to the boil, stirring. Stir in a little sugar if wished and keep warm while you make the puffs.

Cut the butter or margarine into pieces and place in a pan with the water. Place over moderate heat until the butter melts, then bring to the boil and remove from the heat. As soon as the bubbles subside, add the flour, all at once, and beat until the mixture is smooth and leaves the sides of the pan clean. Cool slightly, then beat in the egg yolks, one at a time. Whisk the egg whites until stiff and fold in, then carefully stir in the pasta. Using a tablespoon of mixture to make each puff, deep fry, a few at a time, in moderately hot oil (180°C/360°F) for 1–2 minutes, until crisp and golden brown. Drain well and serve hot, sprinkled with sugar. Serve the warm cherry sauce separately.

Lemon meringue pasta
Serves 4

100 g/4 oz Record pasta caramelle
450 ml/¾ pint milk
1 small can evaporated milk
1 teaspoon ground mixed spices
¾ teaspoon ground cinnamon
2 eggs, separated
2 tablespoons clear honey
4 tablespoons lemon curd
100 g/4 oz castor sugar

Place the pasta, milk, evaporated milk, mixed spices and cinnamon in a saucepan and bring to the boil, stirring. Cover and simmer for about 20 minutes, stirring frequently, until the pasta is soft and the remaining milk liquid creamy. Remove from the heat and beat in the egg yolks and honey.

Divide the lemon curd between 4 ovenproof serving dishes and top with the pasta mixture. Whisk the egg whites until stiff and gradually whisk in the sugar until the meringue is thick and glossy. Spread meringue over the surface of the pasta

Ring puffs with cherry sauce

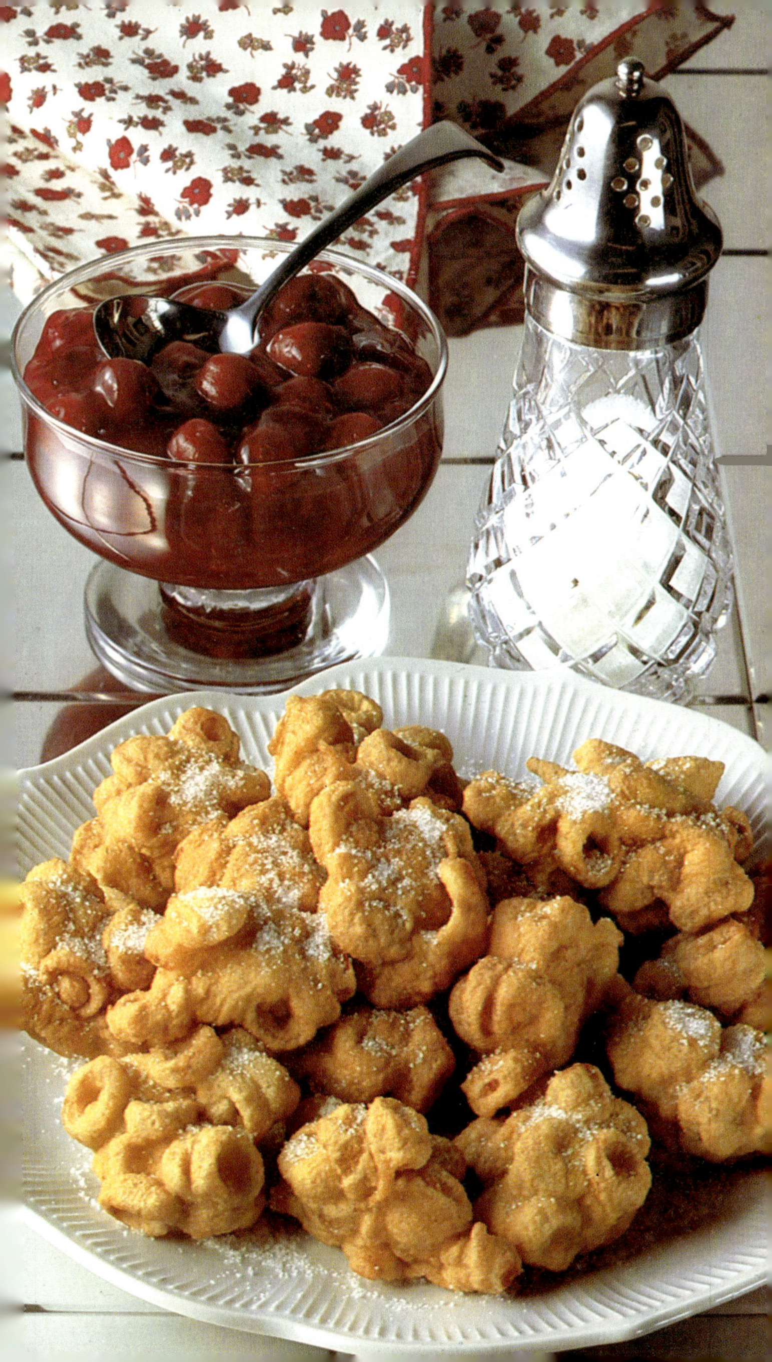

mixture in the dishes, sealing it to the edges. Lift up the top in peaks and bake in a moderate oven (180° C/350°F/Gas Mark 4) for about 15 minutes, or until the peaks are golden brown. Serve immediately.

Jamaican custard pudding ⓠ
Serves 4

75 g/3 oz Record short-cut macaroni
2 tablespoons rum
4 canned pineapple rings
2 bananas, sliced
425 g/15 oz can custard
2 glacé cherries, halved

Cook the pasta in plenty of boiling salted water for 15 minutes, until soft. (This is a little longer than the usual cooking time.) Drain well, sprinkle over the rum, stir well and leave until cold. Place a pineapple ring in the base of each of 4 glass sundae dishes. Mix together the rum flavoured pasta, the banana slices and custard and spoon into the dishes over the pineapple. Decorate each dessert with a cherry half.

Fruited noodle puff
Serves 6

100 g/4 oz Record noodles
100 g/4 oz rhubarb, chopped
2 tablespoons water
225 g/8 oz mincemeat
1 egg, separated
425 g/15 oz can custard
about 3 tablespoons castor sugar

Cook the pasta. Meanwhile, place the rhubarb in a small pan with the water. Cover and cook gently until the rhubarb is tender. Drain the pasta, combine with the rhubarb and juice in the pan, the mincemeat, egg yolk and half the custard. Add a little sugar to sweeten if necessary and transfer to a greased ovenproof pie dish. Whisk the egg white until stiff, add 2 tablespoons of castor sugar and continue whisking until thick and glossy. Fold in the remaining custard and spread over the noodle mixture. Bake in a moderately hot oven (190°C/375°F/Gas Mark 5) for 20 minutes, or until the top is slightly risen and golden brown.

Exotic Puddings and Desserts

Peach upside-down pudding
Serves 6

50 g/2 oz Record short-cut macaroni
300 ml/½ pint milk
75 g/3 oz self-raising flour
2 teaspoons ground cinnamon
150 g/5 oz butter *or* margarine
2 tablespoons golden syrup
75 g/3 oz demerara sugar
425 g/15 oz can peach slices, drained
100 g/4 oz soft brown sugar
2 eggs, separated

Place the pasta and milk in a small pan. Bring to the boil, stirring, then cover and simmer for 25 minutes, stirring frequently, until the pasta has absorbed the milk. Cool.

Line the base of a 20 cm/8 in. cake tin and grease the paper and the tin. Sift the flour and cinnamon together.

Place 25 g/1 oz of the butter or margarine with the syrup and demerara sugar in a small pan and heat gently until melted. Spoon into the lined tin and arrange the peach slices on top. Cream the rest of the fat with the soft brown sugar until light and fluffy. Beat in the egg yolks and the cold pasta mixture, then fold in the dry ingredients. Whisk the egg whites until stiff and fold in carefully.

Spoon over the peach slices in the tin and bake in a moderate oven (180°C/350°F/Gas Mark 4) for about 55 minutes, until well risen and golden brown. Leave in the tin for 5 minutes, then turn out on a serving plate and serve hot or cold.

Honeyed banana noodles

Honeyed banana noodles
Serves 4

225 g/8 oz Record noodles
225 g/8 oz clear honey
grated rind and juice of 2 lemons
100 g/4 oz seedless raisins
50 g/2 oz glacé cherries, halved
50 g/2 oz butter *or* margarine
2 bananas, sliced

Cook the noodles. Meanwhile, put the honey, lemon rind and juice, raisins and cherries into a pan. Heat through gently. Melt the butter in a small frying pan and use to fry the banana slices for 2–3 minutes, until just turning pale golden. Drain the noodles thoroughly, fold in the hot honey sauce and the fried banana and serve hot.

Chocolate macaroni meringue

Serves 4

600 ml/1 pint milk
100 g/4 oz Record quick-cook macaroni
2 tablespoons cocoa powder
1 teaspoon instant coffee powder
2 tablespoons soft brown sugar
2 eggs, separated
100 g/4 oz castor sugar

Reserve 2 tablespoons of the milk and pour the rest into a saucepan. Add the pasta and bring to the boil, stirring. Cook gently for 10 minutes, or until the pasta is tender. Blend the cocoa and coffee with the reserved milk and add to the pan with the sugar. Mix well and bring to the boil, stirring constantly. Remove from the heat and beat in the egg yolks. Divide between 4 ovenproof serving dishes.

Whisk the egg whites until stiff and gradually whisk in the castor sugar until the meringue is thick and glossy. Place in a piping bag fitted with a rose nozzle and pipe rosettes on the pasta mixture. Place in a moderately hot oven (190°C/375°F/Gas Mark 5) for about 10 minutes, or until the tops of the rosettes are golden brown. Serve at once.

Vermicelli ring with rich plum sauce

Serves 4

1 egg, separated
1 egg yolk
75 g/3 oz castor sugar
½ teaspoon ground cinnamon
20 g/¾ oz butter *or* margarine, melted
100 g/4 oz Record vermicelli, cooked
350 g/12 oz ripe plums
125 ml/4 fl oz water
125 ml/4 fl oz sweet sherry *or* Madeira

Whisk the egg yolks with half the sugar until thick, then whisk in the cinnamon and butter or margarine. Stiffly whisk the egg white and fold in with the pasta. Turn the mixture into a well greased 900 ml/1½ pint ring mould and bake in a moderate oven (170°C/325°F/Gas Mark 3) for about 20 minutes, or until firm. Meanwhile, halve and stone the plums.

Place the remaining sugar and the water in a saucepan and stir over gentle heat until the sugar has dissolved. Boil for 10 minutes and stir in the sherry. Add the plums and cook gently for 5 minutes, or until soft. Liquidise the plums and syrup. Turn the vermicelli ring out on a warm serving dish, spoon a little of the warm plum sauce over it and serve the rest in a jug with the pudding.

Banana-berry cream
Serves 4

225 g/8 oz can strawberries
1 strawberry jelly
2 ripe bananas
50 g/2 oz Record pasta shells, cooked
150 ml/¼ pint double cream

Drain the strawberries and make the juice up to 300 ml/½ pint with water. Use to dissolve the jelly, then allow to cool until the mixture is on the point of setting. Slice the bananas and stir into the jelly with the pasta and strawberries. Whip the cream until thick and fold into the strawberry mixture. Turn into a glass serving dish and chill before serving.

Macaroni applecake
Serves 6–8

175 g/6 oz Record short-cut macaroni
900 ml/1½ pints milk
2 dessert apples, peeled
grated rind of 1 lemon
good pinch of ground mixed spices
about 75 g/3 oz castor sugar
75 g/3 oz butter *or* margarine, melted
175 g/6 oz gingernut *or* digestive biscuits, crushed
Decoration
1 red-skinned dessert apple
juice of ½ lemon
150 ml/¼ pint double cream, whipped

Place the pasta in a saucepan with the milk and bring to the boil, stirring. Cover and simmer for about 25 minutes, stirring frequently, until the pasta is soft and has absorbed almost all the milk. Remove the pan from the heat. Grate the apples and stir into the hot pasta mixture with the lemon rind, spices and sugar to taste. Allow to cool, then spoon half into a glass serving dish.

Stir the butter or margarine into the biscuit crumbs and sprinkle most over the pasta mixture in the dish. Top with the remaining pasta mixture and the rest of the crumbs, leaving the centre uncovered. Cut the red-skinned apple into thin slices and dip these in the lemon juice. Pipe a shell border of whipped cream around the top edge of the dish and decorate with apple slices.

Macaroni applecake

CHAPTER 5

SPOTLIGHT ON PASTA PARTIES

All the dinner menus in this section are planned to serve four, but are easy to multiply up to cater for larger gatherings. Pasta makes a star appearance and shows its adaptability as the starter in one menu, the main course in two and a super sweet in yet another. Informal parties, where guests serve themselves with hot dishes from a buffet table, are growing in popularity. With pasta, it is so easy to stretch your budget to serve fun food to a crowd.

Gourmet Dinner Menus

Dinner Party Menu for 4

Melon rafraichi

*Spaghetti with Stilton and bacon

French bean salad

Coffee cream

Melon rafraichi Sprinkle melon wedges with Cointreau or Orange Curaçao and chill.

French bean salad Combine 225 g/8 oz lightly cooked French beans with 2 tablespoons French dressing. Serve sprinkled with 25 g/1 oz toasted flaked almonds.

Coffee cream Dissolve 15 g/½ oz gelatine and 3 tablespoons castor sugar in 300 ml/½ pint double strength hot black coffee. Cool, and when starting to set, fold in 150 ml/¼ pint lightly-whipped double cream. Serve in wine glasses.

Spaghetti with Stilton and bacon

225 g/8 oz Record spaghetti
8 rashers bacon
1 clove garlic, crushed
150 ml/¼ pint single cream
salt and pepper
175 g/6 oz Stilton cheese, crumbled

Cook the pasta. Meanwhile, snip up the bacon and place in a frying pan. Heat gently until the fat begins to run, then add the garlic and fry at a higher heat until the bacon is golden. Drain the spaghetti, stir in the cream, season well and reheat carefully. Fold in the bacon and Stilton and serve at once, piled up on a hot serving dish. Serve with French bean salad.

Dinner Party Menu for 4

Consommé with sherry

Puff pastry fingers

*Mimosa pasta salads

Meringues chantilly

Consommé with sherry Heat 2×425 g/15 oz cans consommé with 4 tablespoons dry sherry to boiling point.

Puff pastry fingers Roll out 225 g/8 oz defrosted frozen puff pastry thinly. Sprinkle one half generously with salt, freshly ground black pepper and a crumbled meat stock cube. Fold over the other half, roll out again to original size, cut into fingers and bake on a damped baking sheet in a hot oven (220°C/425°F/Gas Mark 7) for about 12 minutes, until well risen and golden brown. Serve with the consommé.

Meringues chantilly Put meringue shells together with thick slices cut from block of vanilla ice cream. Serve piped with vanilla-flavoured and sweetened whipped double cream.

Spaghetti with Stilton and bacon; Mimosa pasta salads

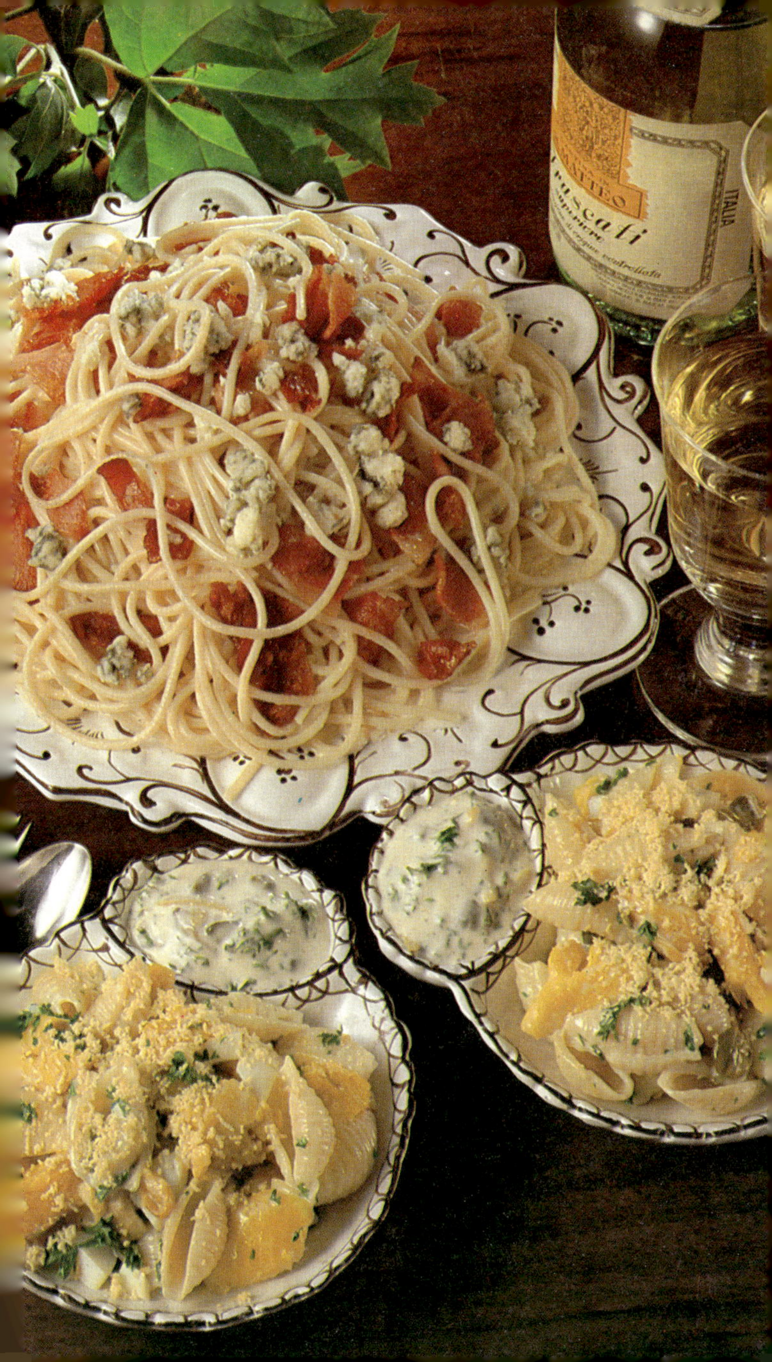
ITALIA

Mimosa pasta salads

225 g/8 oz Record pasta shells
4 tablespoons French dressing
grated rind of 2 lemons
150 ml/¼ pint mayonnaise
2 tablespoons chopped parsley
2 eggs, hard-boiled
225 g/8 oz cooked smoked haddock fillet, flaked
3 tablespoons drained capers
salt and pepper

Cook the pasta, drain well, stir in the dressing and allow to cool, stirring occasionally. Meanwhile, combine the lemon rind, mayonnaise and half the parsley. When the pasta is cold, chop the whites of the eggs and mix with the fish, capers, pasta and remaining parsley. Season to taste and divide between 4 serving dishes. Serve portions of lemon mayonnaise on the side. Sieve the egg yolks over the salads to garnish.

Dinner Party Menu for 4

*Saffron fish shells

Roast lamb with rosemary

Parsnip purée, French beans

Fresh fruit basket

Roast lamb with rosemary Slash the surface of a leg of lamb in diamonds, stick with slivers of garlic and small sprigs of rosemary. Sprinkle with oil and roast.

Parsnip purée Mash cooked parsnip with butter, salt, pepper and ground nutmeg to taste.

Saffron fish shells

225 g/8 oz smoked haddock fillet
450 ml/¾ pint milk
good pinch of saffron strands
½ teaspoon ground turmeric
40 g/1½ oz butter
20 g/¾ oz plain flour
1 tablespoon lemon juice
ground black pepper
1 egg, beaten
50 g/2 oz flaked almonds
175 g/6 oz Record pasta shells, cooked
4 large sprigs parsley

Put the fish in a saucepan, pour over boiling water to cover, allow to stand for 1 minute and drain well. Add the milk, saffron and turmeric to the fish and poach gently for about 15 minutes, until the fish flakes easily when tested with a fork. Remove the fish from the pan, discard skin and bones and flake the flesh roughly. Strain the liquid from cooking the fish and reserve.

Melt two thirds of the butter in the rinsed and dried saucepan, stir in the flour and cook for 1 minute. Gradually add the reserved liquid and bring to the boil, stirring constantly. Add the lemon juice and pepper to taste and simmer for 2 minutes. Beat in the egg and remove the sauce from the heat. Fry the flaked almonds in the remaining butter, until golden. Fold the fish and pasta shells into the sauce and reheat thoroughly but do not allow the sauce to boil. Divide between 4 greased deep scallop shells and garnish with the fried almonds and parsley sprigs.

Penny-wise Entertaining

Buffet Party Menu for 12

*Oven-barbecued sausages with orange twistetti salad

*Curried sausage spaghetti

Lime and avocado jelly

Fresh dates

Lime and avocado jelly Dissolve 3×600 ml/1 pint lime jellies in 900 ml/1½ pints water. Cool and when jelly is syrupy, halve, stone and peel 2 large ripe avocados. Purée with 2 tablespoons lemon juice. Whisk the jelly well and then whisk in the avocado purée. Divide between 12 small sundae dishes and allow to set. Serve decorated with whipped cream.

Oven barbecued sausages with orange twistetti salad

1.5 kg/3 lbs beef sausages
6 tablespoons soy sauce
3 tablespoons Worcestershire sauce
3 tablespoons tomato purée
2 tablespoons made English mustard
3 cloves garlic, crushed
175 g/6 oz clear honey
finely-grated rind of 3 oranges
salt and pepper
Salad
225 g/8 oz Record pasta twistetti, cooked
1 large mild onion, grated
2 large carrots, grated
juice of 3 oranges
salt and pepper

Arrange the sausages on a rack in a roasting tin. Combine the soy sauce, Worcestershire sauce, tomato purée, mustard, garlic, honey and orange rind in a saucepan and stir over gentle heat until well blended. Add salt and pepper if wished. Brush the sausages well with the barbecue sauce and cook in a moderately hot oven (200°C/400°F/Gas Mark 6) for 25 minutes, turning them once during this time and brushing generously with the sauce, until they are a rich golden brown.

Meanwhile, mix together the pasta, onion and carrot for the salad. Pour over the orange juice and season with salt and pepper. Toss the ingredients lightly and serve in a salad bowl with the hot barbecued sausages.

Curried sausage spaghetti

0.75 kg/1½ lbs pork chipolata sausages
2 tablespoons curry powder
3 tablespoons oil
2 medium onions, chopped
1 tablespoon tomato purée
5 tablespoons peanut butter
450 ml/¾ pint beef stock
finely-grated rind and juice of ½ lemon
350 g/12 oz Record spaghetti
salt and pepper
25 g/1 oz salted peanuts, chopped

Twist each sausage in the centre and snip to make 2 smaller sausages. Toss them in the curry powder until coated. Heat the oil and use to fry the coated sausages for about 10 minutes, until cooked through. Drain the sausages and keep hot.

Add the onion to the fat remaining in the pan and fry gently until soft. Stir in the tomato purée, peanut butter, stock, lemon rind and juice and bring to the boil, stirring. Cover and simmer for 15 minutes, stirring occasionally. Meanwhile, cook the pasta, then drain and mix with the sauce. Season the mixture to taste and fold in the sausages. Place on a hot serving dish and sprinkle with the peanuts. Serve hot.

Buffet Party Menu for 12

*Pork and pasta chow

*Sesame chicken

Macaroni crisps (*see* page 9)

Prawn crackers

Gingered pineapple rings

Gingered pineapple rings Drain the syrup from 2 large cans of pineapple rings. Drain the syrup from a 225 g/8 oz jar of preserved ginger and combine with an equal quantity of pineapple syrup. Chop the ginger. Arrange the pineapple rings, overlapping, on a large flat serving dish. Fill the centres with chopped ginger and spoon over the ginger and pineapple syrup.

Pork and pasta chow

2 chicken stock cubes
600 ml/1 pint boiling water
1 tablespoon sugar
2 tablespoons sherry
2 tablespoons vinegar
2 tablespoons soy sauce
1 sweet red pepper
1 sweet green pepper
3 tablespoons oil
2 large onions, sliced
2 large pork fillets (each about 350 g/12 oz)
350 g/12 oz Chinese leaves, shredded
175 g/6 oz canned bamboo shoots, sliced
450 g/1 lb Record pasta caramelle, cooked
1 tablespoon cornflour

Make up the stock cubes with the water and add the sugar, sherry, vinegar and soy sauce. Deseed the peppers and cut them into strips. Heat 2 tablespoons of the oil in a large frying pan and use to fry the onion gently until soft. Push to the sides of the pan and place the pork fillets in the centre. Turn the fillets to seal them on all sides then cover the pan and cook over low heat for 20 minutes, or until the pork is tender. (If liked, sprinkle the pork with Chinese red food powder, which you can buy from a Chinese grocer, or a few drops of red food colouring dissolved in a tablespoon of the stock.) Remove the pork from the pan and keep hot.

Add the remaining oil to the pan with the Chinese leaves and pepper strips. Stir-fry for 3 minutes over high heat and add the bamboo shoots. Heat the cooked pasta in the stock in a large saucepan. Moisten the cornflour with a little water, add to the pasta and bring to the boil, stirring constantly. Simmer for 2 minutes, fold in the vegetable mixture and heat through thoroughly. Turn on to a large serving platter. Slice the pork fillets thinly and arrange the slices overlapping down the centre.

Sesame chicken

0.75 kg/1½ lb boned chicken breasts, cubed
2 tablespoons dry sherry
1 teaspoon salt
¼ teaspoon black pepper
½ teaspoon ground ginger
2 eggs, beaten
4 tablespoons cornflour
4 tablespoons sesame seeds
oil for frying
0.75 kg/1½ lb Record long macaroni
1 bunch spring onions, trimmed
20 cm/8 in. length cucumber, diced

Place the chicken in a shallow dish. Beat together the sherry, salt, pepper, ginger and egg and pour over the chicken. Cover and allow to stand for 30 minutes. Combine the cornflour and sesame seeds in a polythene bag. Add the cubes of chicken, a few cubes at a time, and shake until they are well coated. Deep fry, in batches, in hot oil for about 2 minutes, until golden brown all over. Drain well and keep hot.

Meanwhile, cook the pasta and drain thoroughly. Cut the onions into 2.5 cm/1 in. lengths. Heat 2 tablespoons of oil in a large saucepan and use to toss the onion and cucumber over high heat for 1 minute. Add the pasta, remove the pan from the heat and stir until the pasta strands are coated with oil. Turn on to a warm serving dish and arrange the sesame chicken pieces round the edge.

Sesame chicken; Pork and pasta chow; Macaroni crisps